THE MAN I DIDN'T KNOW

THE MAN
I DIDN'T KNOW

MEIGHAN LEIBERT

NEW DEGREE PRESS

COPYRIGHT © 2023 MEIGHAN LEIBERT

THE MAN I DIDN'T KNOW

ISBN   979-8-88926-815-4   Paperback
          979-8-88926-816-1   Ebook
          979-8-88926-817-8   Hardcover

for family: past, present, and future

my fiercely daring son,

my extraordinarily inspired daughter, and

my paternal Grandma Margaret

CONTENTS

*Everything changes when
I commit myself to the truth.*

AUTHOR'S NOTE

When I was seventeen, a junior in high school, my dad died from alcohol poisoning. Although I understood his drinking to be a problem, his death was a surprise.

What hit me hardest was the impending loss of possibilities. Gone were the future promises I'd imagined for us—particularly, him walking me down the aisle at my wedding and being a grandfather to my not-yet-born children. I was young, a dreamer. His disappearance from my life, in what appeared to be a personal choice, marked me for failure. I was convinced he didn't love me enough to stay alive.

Twenty-three years after his death, I began a search of sorts, inspired primarily by my children. It was my attempt to find, and perhaps understand, the man I didn't know as a child. These pages are filled with inquiry and discovery.

This book is a tribute to my dad and founder of the Berkeley Repertory Theatre (BRT), Michael Williams Leibert.

A box of old papers initiated my quest and overwhelmed me with possibility. It took me another ten years to follow through. I discovered that although he was not an active parent in my life, he was a father to many. Knowing this now gives me comfort. I learned of my dad's generous and creative spirit, his ability to care for, nurture, and stabilize a theater company into being. He was a visionary.

Through his drinking and eventual death, I let my father's absence define me. Feeling worthless made me self-destructive in numerous ways. It wasn't until I was in my fifties that I could acknowledge him for the man he was instead of the father he couldn't be, and I released myself from the pain that trapped me for decades. This is a story of transformation—from insecure daughter to overburdened people pleaser to open-hearted mom.

"Do You Love Me?" by Grandma Margaret

I am afraid of the words.
I go around them as I would a chasm,
or a trap.
I tunnel underneath them
Through ambiguous verbiage,
or fly up to philosophy.
Sometimes I back off,
and retrace my steps.
But then they follow me,
waiting to be spoken.
It would be a simple question,
but it is the answers that I fear.
Every possible answer bearing its own portent;
its weight of pain,
or fragility of rapture.
I do not want to ask.

CHAPTER 1

THINGAMAJIG

Here I am, walking forward into the past.

The warmth of the sun wraps around me like a heavy shawl. It calms my nerves as my sandaled feet sidestep in trepidation. I try to stand sturdy and trust what I've put into motion, but my anticipation is heavier than expected. I'm headed toward my dad's heart, his soul—the Berkeley Repertory Theatre (BRT).

His memorial service was held here twenty-three years ago in 1984 when I was seventeen. Today, I hope to find something more of him for me. My apprehension is due to a needling fear that my efforts are in vain.

It is early September 2007, and the streets of Berkeley are alive with people. Lucky to find parking nearby, I busy myself with unloading the car and getting us situated before we head to the theater. My son Sebastian is thirteen months old and desperate to experience the world, making him eager to run. His curiosity and daring are unstoppable. He is too fast for me these days, so I strap him into his stroller and tuck a blanket around his legs. Fishing into my diaper bag, I pull out a bright green-and-purple plastic thingamajig designed to keep him happy.

My temperature shifts as I stand upright. I put one hand on my belly and pause to slow everything down. I'm in my third trimester, pregnant with my daughter Francesca and call her Frankie for short. I feel immense, heavy, awkward, and achingly full. A cool breeze funnels through the tree-lined street, lifting the hair off my forehead and swirling around the back of my neck. I close my eyes and, for a brief moment, sense all is well. Sebastian kicks his legs and I feel the stroller shift, his signal for us to *move*.

Being a mom gives me the purpose I've been seeking for a long time. I've found a self-expression centered around nurturing. In this new relationship, I am discovering a different language, one that is unspoken. It's not just me or him, or what we do. It's the *love* we create together. It will grow with us and expand when Frankie arrives.

My kids' presence makes me curious about my father. I want to know more about him, to understand the man who wasn't involved in my day-to-day development. My parents divorced when I was five, and I remember very little about my dad. Mom was the primary caregiver; she was the parent who raised me.

The childhood memories surrounding my dad are sparse and disconnected. They arrive in bits and snippets. When I see us together, in a dream or a scene triggered by a photograph, Dad's attention is usually directed toward another.

The frustration from being unseen as a child cornered me like a rat and grew my desperation, leaving me empty inside.

I've carried this vacancy for most of my life, without question. I got used to his unreliability. Hell, maybe I even expected it. But his death changed everything. It stripped me of hope and increased my belief that life is a struggle. Being abandoned by my dad left me rudderless, adrift, and lost.

As a new mom, I am called to claim a sense of my family heritage. I need to step into the world my father left behind and attempt in some way to connect. I've chosen the one place he considered home.

"Recovery" by Grandma Margaret

When I left here it was summer.
Now a new year crawls from winter's womb.
In these long months,
I lay with death beside me;
sometimes as lover,
needed and desirable;
often as foe,
against whose touch I fought with fear.
Now I look long hours
at the peach tree outside my window.
I wonder at the bare, black limbs,
Remembering blossoms, pink and extravagant,
Remembering greening, fruiting, growing,
And feeling it, at last,
Within me, too.

CHAPTER 2

CHOCOLATE CROISSANT

I'm here to find something I lost a long time ago.

I push Sebastian's stroller toward our destination to meet with Susie Medak, managing director of BRT.

A voice starts in my head. *They owe you.*

Not now, I say, worriedly, under my breath.

The voice continues. *Your dad is dead because of them. They forced him out.*

That's an intense accusation. I keep pushing the stroller forward. The street is flat, but it feels as though I am going uphill.

Silence.

The voice seems to be waiting for me to say something. So, I say meekly, *If I lead with that, I will get nowhere fast.*

More silence.

He deserved better, it says.

Of course he deserved better. And here we are without him.

Looking down at my son, I try to shake off these needy thoughts. Sebastian is mangling the toy with his mouth, and his shoeless toes are curled in delightful concentration. He prefers to be barefoot, and I admire how his feet reflect his mood. I suppose mine do too; I just never noticed before. For a long time, I covered up my feet because I thought they were ugly. Twelve years ago, I wanted to have a new experience around the parts of my body that kept me moving all day long and decided, essentially, to see them as beautiful. Now I, too, enjoy being barefoot whenever possible.

Be positive. Be open, I think.

"Meighan?" a lovely woman says, waving her arm toward me as I stroll the three of us into the main lobby. "I'm Susie. I'm so glad to meet you." She's good looking with stunningly thick, blond, curly hair.

Envy and admiration swirl together as I smile back. "Me too. Thanks so much for making time for me." I look down at my son and add, "Well, us," I offer enthusiastically.

Susie spins me around, and we're out the same door we entered moments before. In front of me she turns her head slightly to ask, "How far along are you?"

"I'm seven months now," I say proudly. "Her name is Francesca. Her nickname will be Frankie, but who knows what will happen. I had dreams of calling my son Ash, and I'm still committed to three syllables," I giggle. "Sebastian is a mouthful, and it works for me and him, I think."

We walk up the street to a café, choosing a table outside. We're on a slight incline, so I have to secure the stroller by locking the wheels. Bending over isn't easy, and coming up makes me dizzy. As I take a seat across her and am distracted by my squirming son, my nervousness moves toward regret. *Maybe this was a mistake.* I'm extremely warm and a little thirsty. Beads of sweat dot my forehead.

A young girl with short, pink hair and a nose ring appears to take our order. We opt for beverages and baked goods. When she walks away, I smile at Susie, flooded with doubt. *What the hell am I doing here?*

Sebastian punctuates the air around us with short squeals of discontent. I suspect he wants release from his stroller.

"Sorry," I say to Susie. "I know full well if I set him free, all bets are off." I shuffle through my purse and pull out a ring of keys, my sunglasses, and a small hand mirror. "This will keep you busy." I hand him the goods and briefly admire his brown curly hair dappled with sunlight as his long-lashed, gray eyes beam over the trinkets I deliver.

Susie smiles at me and then looks to Sebastian. We talk of the weather, my pregnancy, the demands of motherhood, and almost anything else other than my dad until our drinks and food arrive. I give Sebastian a chocolate croissant, and he grabs onto it, pulling the soft bread toward his face. *His actions are direct and clear.*

Once he's engaged, I relax a bit. Susie peers at me with a look that says, "How may I help you?" Her welcoming face softens my nerves, and I'm encouraged by her cheerfulness. Or is it something else? Being with her makes me feel energized in a way. *Was my dad like you? Kind and inspired?*

"I'm looking to reconnect with people who knew my dad," I finally spit out. It's as close to the truth as I can get. I can't find the words to ask for what I want, to be included in the theater somehow. Sitting across from her, the fantasy of thinking I belong to BRT begins to surface. It envelops me like the hug from a long-lost brother. *That's it*, I think. *We're family.*

Is this the jealousy I knew so well as a kid? It simmers deep, an old story sparked long ago. My dad never had time for me. I want to be held in some way by the theater. Invited back into the fold because, like me, it was once his baby.

I let my thoughts run wild while smiling and chewing. Is it possible? Lifetime Subscriber Status, is that a thing? Can I get that? This is a dream I've been carrying for years. *No, I feel owed.* The minute I think this, my mouth goes dry. I swallow a few times as I sadly imagine Susie opening her arms to me and whispering, "Welcome home, dear Meighan."

Susie graciously admits she never knew my dad personally and pulls a pen from her purse to write on a paper napkin. She hands me a list of contacts. Some of the names are familiar. *Would anyone remember me?*

"We found a box in the attic while cleaning things out," she tells me. "Looks like some of your dad's papers," she adds while we finish up our coffees. "Come with me, and you can take a look."

My head is spinning with all the possibilities of what could be in that box. I am unable to make small talk and choose to stay quiet. When we enter the lobby, I settle into my surroundings. Transported back in time, everything looks the same, just as I remember from when I was a teenager. A strange sensation runs through me, a feeling of home that makes me a little sad. The walls are speaking to me, and I hear them say, "Where have you been? Yes, I know you."

The foyer is open and spacious with high ceilings. Sunlight filters through the courtyard doors highlighting the hallway leading to the bar, Michael's Second Act. A hanging neon sign points the way, and I laugh gently to myself. *Well, Dad, look at that. Now we can have a drink together.*

"Wait here a minute," Susie says, moving away from me. "I'll be right back." She walks through a door and disappears.

It's quiet. Sebastian's stroller wheels squeak along the hardwood floors. The concession stand is empty, a lonely counter yearning for attention. *I know the feeling.* Looking through the glass doors, my eyes scan the courtyard. I see tables with chairs and the outdoor staircase leading to the upper level. It's a larger and more spread-out version of the original theater he founded in 1968 on College Avenue. Upstairs holds the green room, BRT offices, costume design and dressing rooms—Dad's other home.

My brick is out there.

"Buy-A-Brick" was a successful fundraising campaign developed by Carolyn Kemp in the late '70s to support the building of the new theater. Dad bought one each for me and my brother, where he cemented us into the courtyard. Forever. *Oh, Dad, why did you have to die?*

"August 5th Memoriam" by Grandma Margaret

You are laid there
in the familiar, yellow shirt,
Faintly smiling, but much too still.
I speak your name,
And silence answers.
I touch your arm,
You are not there.
Empty embodiment of being,
Living in memory, and dreams,
Marking the minds and faces of my children,
Speaking through words my own voice
speaks today;
Where are you now,
Incorporate, vanished father?
Are you aware of our remembering?

CHAPTER 3

COLLEGE AVENUE LIQUOR

Just as I am remembering Dad, he appears.

A giant black-and-white photograph hangs on the far wall, calling me forward. *It's him. He's here.* I am surprised, and my body stiffens. Tiny electric sparks travel beneath my skin and make me dizzy. I lean on the handlebars of Sebastian's stroller so I don't lose my balance. How is it possible a photograph can illicit such deep emotions? Flooded with grief, loneliness, and thrill is too much. It's been so long since I've felt him this close.

Sadness swirls around my insides and crashes against my heart. Sebastian and I squeak closer to find an entire wall designed in dedication. "Michael Williams Leibert...In loving memory...Founder..." I read.

"This is your grandpa," I say to Sebastian as I point my finger toward the photo.

I am glued to Dad's eyes. Soaking him in, my gaze meanders along his smile, his beard, his hand resting on his shoulder. Here he is, so close and so far away at the same time. I read the words written here that describe the man whose vision brought this theater to life. *Where are you, Dad?*

"Here it is," Susie says brightly, jolting me back to reality. I am not ready to leave him.

Looking over my left shoulder, I watch Susie move closer and listen to her shoes snap along the flooring. She hands me a full box with a lid. Her gesture is final. *Why would we look through it together?*

It's heavy in my hands, like a secret treasure. I wiggle it underneath Sebastian's seat. *What will I find inside? A lost manuscript? Oh, how I would so appreciate a letter, something from him to me.*

"I'm sorry I couldn't give you more," Susie adds, waving as she turns. A pang of embarrassment washes over me and has me thinking I've taken up too much of her time.

Sebastian and I move toward the exit. I say, smiling, "Goodbye and thanks so much for your help." Pushing open the door and walking out into the sunlight, I consider the space between *now* and *then*. Maybe it's too late for me to reconcile his death.

My heart is pounding in my chest. The rush of adrenaline makes me a little queasy. I gaze up at the sky and wonder if Dad is looking down on us.

I slide the box onto the passenger side first and then move Sebastian to his car seat and stash the stroller in the trunk.

Squeezing myself behind the wheel, I take a moment to be still. Closing my eyes, I say to no one in particular, "Okay. Here I go." I reach my hand under the lid and pull out two pieces of paper. I see my dad's familiar signature drawn from a fountain pen with blue ink. *God, how he loved those pens.*

As I focus my gaze and drink in what I am seeing, I laugh softly and squeeze out a few tears while doing so. I'm holding two written checks from the Berkeley Repertory Theatre special account made out to College Avenue Liquor. One dated September 11, 1977, for twenty dollars and the other dated September 12, 1977, for ten dollars.

Maybe Dad isn't so hard to find after all.

"Here and Now" by Grandma Margaret

Stranger to yesterday
and tomorrow,
This moment is all I know of you,
And all there is of me.
Change is certain.
Expectation treacherous.
So let us know the present,
which was, and is, and will be.

CHAPTER 4

CLIMBING

I need to get home.

I take a beat. My stress begins to build like an electric charge. I know this feeling well. It has me thinking I'm not doing enough and usually pushes me forward at an unreasonable pace.

I'm nervous and uncomfortable, partly ashamed for wanting something from BRT and also sad not having my dad. The discomfort forces me into judgment, and I start criticizing myself. It's unconscious enough so I am not aware of it but leaves me with a strong urge to run and get somewhere else. *Sebastian needs to be home napping,* I tell myself.

The impact of wanting more connection to my past is overwhelming. I sit with what's left of Dad next to me and, instead of fleeing, attempt to realize what is here.

"I did it," come the words in a whisper. "I got something—a whole box and a few names. Be happy."

Happy?

"Okay, then, how about satisfied?" I hear and refuse to answer.

Instead, I say, *Sebastian does not need to sleep at home. He can nap in the car. Stop making everything so complicated.*

Reaching into the diaper bag, I hand my son a bottle of formula. He takes it happily. Our breast-feeding days were short lived. I'll never forget that visit with the pediatrician when she told me gently, "Your son is not gaining weight." No mother wants to hear those words.

I pumped multiple times a day because somebody told me it would generate more breastmilk. *Well, it didn't.* I followed the rules, did what I was told, and my son was starving. Anxiety had me in a tailspin. *I was inadequate.*

Immediately and begrudgingly, I resigned myself to powdered milk so my boy would grow. And he did. Sebastian quickly got thick and plump. It turned out to be an easy solution.

His appetite only increased thereafter. The garden apartment was the perfect place to start our family. Fruit trees lined our front yard: plum, pear, and apple. Sebastian would crawl in the dirt and eat the fallen fruit off the ground. Watching him was satisfying in those moments, where life seemed filled with shallow pockets of easy and simple.

That first year I made all of Sebastian's baby food from scratch. I wore pregnancy and motherhood as a second skin, like my freckles—close and familiar. I created beautiful food for my child, filled with nutrition and flavor, and my son ate everything I put in front of him. One of my dreams was to introduce him to as many delicacies as possible, to broaden his palate early on. Homemade felt wholesome and pure.

Sebastian's appetite for life is strong. Vitality pours out of his little being, making him determined in everything he does—even now, as he finishes his bottle and falls asleep. His head drops to the left slightly, sun warming his face through the window, and he naps. Following the rise and fall of his chest slows me down, and I surrender myself to love.

I turn my attention back to Dad and smile. *I will deal with you later.* Driving home I place my right hand on the lid, letting him know I'm here. *What am I going to do with you?*

Pulling the car into the driveway, I park. Sebastian continues to sleep. We've only been driving for twenty-three minutes, and I hope to keep him down for another hour. I'm willing to try and gently carry him to his crib. *So far, so good.*

I grab the box out of the car and prepare myself for some digging. I sit on the floor with what's left of my dad in front of me and gather handfuls of paper at a time. I come across bank statements, more checks, notecards, letters, and numerous employment contracts from various theater companies—remnants of his life, each a thread of a different story, together in a box.

People wrote excerpts from plays and poetry in their communications with him. I get dizzy with the fantastic truth that sits in front of me. My dad communicated through the language of poets and writers. The sensitivity alone is a beautiful surprise.

I sit with these forgotten memories, glimpses from a past that mostly still unsettle me, and find myself swimming in the unknown. Or is it? I too am romantic at heart. Why am I surprised to find such eloquent details surrounding Dad? Questions flood my brain as I try to wrap sense around the confusion that swaddled me as a child. *Did you speak to me in poetry? Why were you so busy all the time? I mostly only remember you walking away.*

Sebastian's wail brings me back to the present; he cries to let me know he is done napping. When I carry him from the crib, I glance at the pile of papers strewn across the floor and think, *What a mess.*

I change Sebastian's diaper, and the minute his feet hit the ground, he's off. I cherish his curiosity. He moves toward the built-in bookshelves. He's a climber. "Where are you going?" I whisper.

He is not deterred by my voice. He's smiling as I watch his toes push against the wooden edge to carry him higher. His fingers grip a shelf from above to pull him upward, balance and strength in motion.

Fear and concern are present. *Be careful. Don't fall. Beware of the books*, I think. I don't want to assume the worst, nor do I want to prevent him from knowing his own capabilities.

"Double Life" by Grandma Margaret

Waking, dozing
I drag heavily between two worlds.
My sleep is peopled with the past.
Father, children
A long forgotten friend
Returning now in jest or anger,
To haunt my dreams like a shadow
that dissolves with the day.
Waking, I am alone, alone.
The house rattles with remembrance,
And I am closed tight, like a purse,
Over the voices of the night.

CHAPTER 5

SHY

I lovingly watch my son tackle the bookshelves with a twang of envy. I'm enjoying his daring, wishing I had more of my own. What was it like for my parents? Did they watch me with the same appreciation?

Remembering Dad hurts. He wasn't the only one to leave. I also lost my paternal grandma along with all my aunts and uncles. Maybe that's what death does; it just strips you bare. One minute we were gathering for holiday dinners and birthdays, and the next minute—*poof*—we weren't. I identify with being abandoned on purpose.

I took his death personally and believed he chose the bottle over me. *Now there's some daring.* How bold I was to presume I could wield power as a daughter. My understanding of love as a child was confused. His passing gave me cause; I wanted people to feel sorry for me. Sympathy is love. That's what I know.

Thoughts push down on my eyebrows, descending weight to my teeth so I clench them tightly. Stress is here. Pain.

No, not now. Rubbing my thumbnail in circular motions with the tip of my index finger on both hands gently eases me out from the haze of remembering.

Sebastian deftly works his way down from the height of the shelves. As he moves toward a basket of blocks, sadness overwhelms me. Mom often tells me how she used to leave me crying in my crib for hours. She's not proud and is burdened with regret. She would close the door and walk away, unsure of what else to do. I was unmanageable. *I will not do this to my children.*

Sebastian pulls the basket onto its side, spilling the contents across the carpeted floor. I admire his focus; he appears so intent and happy with what he is doing. I send a quiet prayer toward the heavens that my children always choose for themselves what feels right and that as their mother, I provide them enough space to flourish.

My son, done with the blocks, walks toward me and climbs into my lap. His meaty fingers play with my necklace while I kiss his forehead and hug him close. My eyes travel to the pile of papers on the floor and I see the word "Memorial" written on an envelope. I reach down and bring it closer. I open the envelope to see printed on UC Berkeley Drama Department letterhead the memorial speech written by William Oliver in 1984.

I hold it gently and catch my breath, worried my attention might dissolve its presence as I begin to read...

We are here because, in one way or another, most of us have had the pleasure of knowing Michael Leibert. I doubt, however, if any two of us had the same pleasure or knew Michael in precisely the same way...and this fact alone says something about the mercurial talent and shy gentleman that he was. I am here today to bear witness to the four words in the description I've just given him: shy, talent, gentleman and mercurial.

I first knew Michael as a graduate student. He was mature beyond his years, virile, and possessed of a lovely voice! A university theater director's dream... at last! Someone able to play a honcho leading role! I promptly cast him in the honcho role of all time: Horace in the play of the same name by Corneille. Then I first discovered what a truly gentle man Michael was and what a mercurial actor he could be.

I was surprised to discover it was difficult for him to achieve the ruthless severity and violence of Horace. I recall how he struggled from rehearsal to rehearsal, steeling himself to respond to the famous attack made on Horace by his sister (who was played by Dana Evans). Michael succeeded. He gave us the rage and committed the murder, which I had placed on the stage rather than in the wings, as is traditional, so there would be no cheating. However, Dana and I knew how difficult it was for him. His problem in playing Horace sprang from one of his most endearing aspects: his gentleness and his kindness. I saw Michael, on more than one occasion, vent anger upon himself rather than inflict unpleasantry upon others.

This gentleness and kindness are closely related to his loyalty and generosity. I'm sure the actors in the audience today need no reminder of Michael's altogether rare courage in the loyalty with which he supported actors...not just as performers but as people worthy of respect and in need of confidence. He was loyal to you, and he attempted to be your friend...at the same time he endeavored to be your employer and director...a very difficult mix for a shy and gentle artistic director.

I've called Michael shy, and those of you who knew him primarily as a public figure may question the appropriateness of my description. But I recall several occasions in which I observed Michael "fronting" for his theater, and although he was genial, warm, and urbane, I was always aware of a tense privacy hidden behind the eye...something akin to the trepidation I had detected in his eyes during his rehearsals of Horace. This private tension was, in my opinion, related to his gentlemanliness. I have heard actors demand stronger more intrusive coaching from Michael...and I realized the integrity of that private self made him pause before intruding into the privacy of another. Having overcome his protective restraint, Michael was capable of courageous honesty and an almost confessional openness.

I directed Michael in one of the last roles he played in this theater. He chose the play for himself A Life in the Theatre *by David Mamet. He was afraid of the role... a fact that simply emphasized the confessional bravery and honesty of his choice. Even learning lines seemed difficult for him this time. Throughout the rehearsal I had the certainty that the difficulty he was experiencing was not technical in its origin but, rather, the result of forcing a self-confrontation within the role.*

If the struggle to make himself over into the violent severity of Horace had been difficult, playing the older actor in A Life in the Theatre *was fearsome. But Michael again succeeded and delivered himself what I consider to be one of the more moving performances of his career. I will never forget the day we blocked the scene in which the older actor hangs about the theater eavesdropping on the younger actor's rehearsal of a tryout soliloquy. I asked Michael to lurch in from various entrances and vomitoria...including that door up there in the back that issues from the office. The effect I wanted, I said to him, was of this old actor who can't pull away...haunting both theater and the career of the younger actor. He played the scene masterfully... in a way I shall never forget...and if the direction I gave him upon that occasion proves to be prophet I can't wish this theater a gentler, kindler, more talented and benevolent ghost to haunt it.*

The first line hits me hard. I cannot say I had the pleasure of knowing my dad.

Who is this man being described? I am genuinely intrigued and surprised. All this time, I've spent my life sandwiched between a dad who was too busy and a dad who died. With this loving testimony to his character, talent, and generosity, I am uncomfortably proud.

Gentle and kind and loyal. *My dad?* All of this seems so far from my own experience of him. I taste new flavors, sweet and fruity. I swallow bitterness too and detect a hint of anger.

This is a new outline, giving me a different picture. Dad was human. He loved, he feared, he dared, he triumphed, he risked. This is the man Mom fell in love with. And this is also a man I didn't know—here, in black and white.

Sebastian, heavy in my lap, squirms to be let down. I put him on the floor, and he moves to the nearest toy, which appears to be the empty box that held my father. I see my son's mind working out all the possibilities, and I leave him to it.

Leaning back, my eyes close to give me space. In one hand, I grasp the thrill of discovery, touching history between my fingertips. In the other I clench the pain of loss, closely knit with my sense of worth as I let it fill me with doubt. The torment is too big. I allow the abandonment I've been carrying for decades to envelop me. *He is gone. I wasn't enough to keep him alive. What do I hope to accomplish now? What would my knowing more provide?*

Under the weight of discouragement, I imagine myself slipping beneath water, moving slowly in one direction, as the light from above disappears and the dark from below swallows me whole. I cringe at the thought of contacting my father's colleagues and friends. *What would I say exactly?*

Sebastian climbs inside the box. He's raising the lid above his head. I laugh out loud and think, *No, dear one. Stay free.*

Frankie kicks. I put my hand to the right of my belly to feel her do it again. *Yes.* I choose my children. Gathering all the papers, I place them in a drawer at the bottom of my desk and close it.

I am not ready.

"Mute" by Grandma Margaret

Enough that the days are strange,
And that this house is full of ghosts.
The quiet roars around me,
Echoing words from another time.
Reflections distort my room
to some place subtly unfamiliar,
and in the mirror I see a face
lined with calligraphy of the past.
I try to write;
Reaching for that which steadies
In a wavering reality;
For words that translate one life to another,
the past to the present.
Enough that I know not where I am.
Too much to lose
The only voice I have for crying out.

CHAPTER 6

WAITING

Am I ever ready?

So many of my big moments seem to fall apart and morph into something else. What appears to be constant in these situations is my emotional immaturity. Sections of me are stunted, making me petty and unkind.

I remember my marriage ceremony and being asked to envision two rings, slightly overlapping. "The space in the middle is shared. It signifies the two of you together. The other spaces represent you as individuals. Keep the balance between the three for a strong union. Always maintain a sense of who you are," the Reverend said brightly. "Be clear on yourself."

My negative reaction to these words stemmed from misunderstanding. *What was the Reverend talking about?* I was getting married to change who I was inside, and my belonging to another would make me better. As I saw it, my ring was directly below my husband's with no overlapping shared section. Together, we were one.

The day after our wedding, I was still me. This was an unfortunate surprise. Maybe having a baby would fix me?

And a year later I was pregnant at forty. It was a miracle.

It is late December, a holiday weekend for gathering with cheer, and we are visiting friends, soon-to-be godparents, at their home up north. Alcohol doesn't taste good to me, and I remove myself from the festivities to pee on a stick. I've never been so happy to see a plus sign. For the full two minutes it takes me to find the others, I'm the only one who knows.

We chose his name immediately. I wave the test results in my hand and exclaim with full force, "We're pregnant." I walk outside to join the others, seated around a roaring fire.

"Sebastian!" my husband says with the beaming smile of a little boy.

"What if it's a girl?" I throw back at him, unsure of how to respond and biding my time.

"Then we name her Sebastiana," he says sipping his beer.

"Why this name?" I ask. I don't like it. It sounds typical to me, boring, unimaginative. I want my son's name to sound dynamic and exciting. *Or maybe I just want to have some input.* Already, I begin to think of myself as doing all the work.

"My parents said they were considering this name for me when I was born," he says, as if to explain.

"Really?" I question. "So you want to name our child the name you didn't get?" This seems strange, like eating scraps of food that had originally been thrown away.

"Yes, I do," he says excitedly. "It'll be like having two of me."

"This is our baby. His name needs to be spectacular!" I shout in return, a little embarrassed by my volume.

"Yes," he says again. "Sebastian."

I surrender unwillingly and begin designing my own list for middle names. I remember this story as if it were yesterday. The onset of our parenting, together and separated at the same time.

Today I love my son's name. It grew on me, and I honestly can't imagine a better moniker for him. Now, I am a mother with a second child on the way. All my dreams are coming true. Here we are, a family, and I still feel empty inside, like something is missing. It scares me so I ignore it as much as possible and pretend it isn't here.

Like clockwork, I stir myself awake. It's 4:00 a.m. I am oblivious to the constriction in my body, the tightness around my chest that compels me to go faster. It's like I am continuously running away from what is here, driven by an urgency to get somewhere else. My movements are abrupt and quick, a habit of doing that has been with me for a long time.

I check on Sebastian, and he's fast asleep. He reminds me of a snow angel, all splayed out. No, maybe he's a starfish. *It doesn't matter*. He is uncovered and open, available. *I have no idea what that feels like*. I lift the colored fabric scrunched in the corner of his crib and slide it over his body to keep him warm in the chill of the morning.

I use the time to bathe. Relaxing and going slowly is not my strong suit. Even now, I feel compelled to rush, to prepare in some way for the unexpected. I consider a washcloth for my pits and privates. Resisting the temptation to speed through the process, I let the shower run. Steam fogs up the mirror, and I swipe my hand across the glass, distorting my reflection. It's impossible for me to see what is here. I've been ignoring myself for too long. I recognize my green eyes, freckled complexion, and rich brown hair as the makings of an imposter. I stay cloaked and covered, blinded by an unconscious desire to be something better, anything other than myself.

Stepping into the shower I let the hot water slide over my body. It feels good to be alone. I go through my to-do list for the day before the sun rises and use it to make me ready.

Routine is dependable. It holds me together, my best friend. Getting up early has been my way for decades. Morning dark excites me with the reality of getting things done before the day has officially begun. I consider myself efficient, and it is one of the lies I tell myself.

Pre-dawn is the time of day where I do my best cleaning, organizing, exercising, and planning.

After my shower I sit to meditate for twenty minutes. I watch my thoughts speed around me like ants and give them attention, faking my stillness.

Consumed by my thinking, I have little space for quiet. My desperation to feel loved has me fleeing from what is here. On the inside I am insecure and scattered, but on the outside I am confident and focused. I wear my hiding like a badge of courage to get through my day.

My self-hatred is everywhere, coursing through my blood, my bones, and seeping through the pores of my skin, blanketing me like a shield. My unawareness prevents me from understanding I am always alone and scared. I can't admit it to myself or anyone else. Neither marriage nor motherhood removed these torturous bedfellows from my life.

I repeat under my breath, "I do everything, and he doesn't appreciate me," when I clean the house, do the laundry, make the food, go to the park, go to the grocery store, go to the park again, and even when I visit my mom to drop Sebastian off for a sleepover. I am consumed with my incessant thinking. I am a woman determined—undervalued, unsatisfied, and unhappy.

I rationalize, since I've been awake since 4:00 a.m., I cannot be held responsible for my thoughts. I ride the wave without question.

Waiting for my husband to return home from work is never easy. Paralyzed with fear I convince myself something terrible happened as it is the only explanation for his nonresponse.

This is another ritual of mine: getting tied up in knots over something imagined.

It is late afternoon, 4:30 p.m., and I have my hand around my belly.

"Frankie," I murmur, "where is your father?"

With my forehead pressed against the glass, I watch my breath fog up the window as I exhale. My eyes blur as they penetrate the rose bushes in the garden. I look at their living beauty and the fallen petals blanketing the soil beneath them. They are resplendent bits from the whole, nourishing the seeds to come.

I am stunned into a different kind of stillness, filled with rumination, and stuck in a cycle.

I wait.

None of our conversations make a difference. No matter how much I beg him to care, to be different, to consider my feelings, nothing changes. Every single day I am consumed with worry. His inattention makes my crazy. I think of ways to retaliate, to give him a taste of his own medicine.

I'll hide and pretend I'm not here so he can come home and wonder where I am!

I walk my belly through the apartment to find the perfect spot. Standing in our bedroom, I settle my gaze toward the corner of the room. I slide myself between the end of my son's crib and the wall, pull the bureau close, and cover us with a blanket. *If I fall asleep, I can stay here for hours.*

My head is churning, spilling out one negative thought after another. The revving in my system has me fully charged. My eyes close and I beg my body to relax, but the thoughts are unrelenting. *He's out with friends...or drinking with colleagues...having fun while I sit here alone...why doesn't he care...maybe he got in an accident...or a car clipped his bike when he was riding home from the ferry in the dark?*

I hate feeling forgotten.

Now 6:30 p.m. My commitment has me here for two hours. I don't have any messages on my phone. I am angry and frustrated.

I unbury myself and rearrange the furniture. I am deeply embarrassed and mortified by my—*what is it*—payback? Is that what I'm doing? Shame creeps along my skin, and I shiver in response. *What is wrong with me? What does it mean to feel foolish alone when nobody else gets to see?*

In the kitchen I cook my way through discomfort to keep busy. I open the fridge and pull ingredients for avocado and tomato salad with green onion, roasted rack of lamb with garlic, rosemary, and mashed potatoes.

8:15 p.m. "Hi honey, I'm home," he says lightly, walking through our front door. I recognize his pleasant manner and cringe with disgust. His ease is infuriating. Our front door opens into the kitchen. Seated in the living room, tense with anger and brooding, I listen to him poking around and making a plate of food. I rise to greet him.

"Where the hell have you been? Why don't you answer your phone or call to tell me what's up with you? Didn't you get my messages? Any of them? My head goes to crazy places! I imagine you lying in a ditch. Don't you understand? I grew up with this shit! Why can't you communicate?" He doesn't even look at me, placing his plate on the table and pouring himself a glass of wine.

"Meighan," he finally says. "I'm here, okay? Everything is fine." He smiles up at me from his seat at the table, enjoying his meal.

No. No, it's not.

"Generations Gap (to McGurrin)"
by Grandma Margaret

I sat in the warm sun,
Holding my first son's first son in my arms.
Past and present blurred; and then
Freed from each other by all the years between,
I smiled at him with only love,
And he smiled back at me.

CHAPTER 7

INDUCED

My living unhappily goes unnoticed. I'm too busy being nine months pregnant and managing a toddler. I let the demands of motherhood distract me from the truth of my marriage. I have a long history of pushing, obsessively, to get what I want. Only sometimes does it work out to be something I need.

I remember the first time I tried Bikram yoga, a series of twenty-six postures with two breathing exercises, practiced in a room lined with mirrors and warmed to 105-degree heat. Mary Jarvis was my first teacher, and it took me months to get through an entire class without lying down. "Just do what you can," she'd tell me. "In time, you will grow stronger."

I didn't like Savasana, known as "corpse pose," a place for integration and recovery. I had no relationship with care at this time in my life, and doing nothing felt unreasonable. It would take me another ten years to understand that movement is medicine for the body, and stillness is medicine for the mind.

After two years of regular practice, I asked Mary about teacher training. I did not have a dream of becoming an instructor. I only hoped to deepen my understanding of yoga philosophy, or at least that's what I told myself. What I really wanted was to change my life. In 2002, I completed Bikram yoga teacher training in Los Angeles with 304 other students. Because I quit my job to attend the nine-week program and sublet my apartment, I began asking for work at any Bikram studio that would hire me. I slowly built a career and reputation, traveling throughout the Bay Area.

I practiced and taught yoga through both my pregnancies. Being in a hot room was like home for me. I was focused and determined and intense. Mary would tell us in class, "I love you." My whole body changed when I heard these words. *Am I lovable?* It was ninety minutes of being with me and showing my teacher I was invested. Acceptance was slowly incoming, but it started in the hot room. Mary would remind me often, "It's a process, Meighan. It takes time." *Ain't that the truth.*

The sterile environment of my obstetrician's office is cold. I distract myself by decorating. I see brightly colored tapestries and cozy fabrics lining the walls. While he's busy scoping my insides I tell him, imploringly, "She needs to be born on the twenty-ninth. My husband leaves on the first of November, and she can't be late."

"Where's he going again?" he asks distractedly.

"Lansing, Michigan," I begin. "An emergency project, a bridge collapse. He'll go ahead of us. I don't want to travel with a newborn. I told him we will show up for Christmas," I say, with dread. I don't want to move all the way across the country for a year.

"Induce her," he says. "That's your easiest solution. There's no guarantee she will arrive naturally when you expect her."

Don't I know it, I think. I pretend to forget my own history with expectations. And then, of course, I remember.

On Sebastian's due date, I waited, patiently, forever. Clearly, my son had other plans. I sat with him keenly coaxing. "C'mon, let's do this!" And the more I thought about it, the more I realized he might just be so happy inside, safe. *I wouldn't want to come out either.*

The next day, I feigned disinterest. I acted as though I weren't pregnant—if that's even possible at forty-two weeks. I woke up, got dressed, and pretended to forget how I'd spent the last forty-eight hours so excited for his arrival.

Full bellied, I drove to a music festival to meet my cousin Nadine. Our moms are sisters. Nadine grew up in Big Sur, a small beach town south of Carmel. I loved visiting her when we were kids. Her mom had an amazing house high on a hill. We would go to the beach every day and play in the waves. We were young, wild, and free.

Now we were adults living in Marin County. Being with her in the park and enjoying live music reminded me of the fun we used to share.

"How are you feeling?" she asked. Nadine was a bright light in my life, always down for a groove. She epitomized joy. This woman was like a party and full of love. Being with her was a welcome distraction from my son not arriving on time.

"Great. This is the way to invite Sebastian into the world. Let's show him all the fun that awaits!" I screamed over the sound of the music.

Washington Square Park was small, nestled in the heart of North Beach of San Francisco, the neighborhood that held me as a child. All the music festival vendors were lined up along the edge of the grass like train cars. Nadine bought me an orange cowboy hat to save my face from sunburn, but it was too late. My shoulders were red too, and none of it mattered.

Being there was amazing. Sitting outside under the blue of the sky and the shine of the sun with live music surrounding us felt like magic.

I spread my arms wide and twirl. *Freedom. Life. Beauty.* Tasting it in that moment gave me hope. I'd been pretending not to care for hours, but of course I did. I walked myself to the shade of a giant tree and swallowed hard. The truth was I didn't want to go home.

My thoughts began to simmer as I drove. They became a rolling boil when I crossed the Golden Gate Bridge. No calls...no texts...nothing from the father of my child, all day long. Did he even miss me or ever wonder where I was? I continued to exert my independence while being tethered to the belief I was not loved.

I had my own blinders on, preventing me from acknowledging what was happening in my marriage. My pain reduced me to reacting and complaining. Consumed by fear and doubt, I kept thinking my husband didn't care.

Is this survival—not getting what I want, encased in a shroud of blame? I unconsciously held onto this state of being like it was a life preserver, afraid of who I would be without it. This was who I was the day before my son entered the world.

His was a long birth, almost ten hours. And as scared as I was, I found courage to lock the door and keep a doctor I didn't like away from my body to let nobody tell me what I couldn't do. My son showed me how to pay attention and listen, something he would continue to do throughout his life.

Today, fifteen months later, the urgency surrounding the birth of my daughter is unwelcome. My needing her to get here on time feels insane. *But what can I do?*

I get the shot of Pitocin at 9:00 a.m. The process intrigues me—clean and undramatic. I am told, with the prick of a needle, labor contractions will start within an hour. The whole scene appears dreamy until it's not. I get nervous. *What have I done? Maybe I shouldn't have pushed for this. Let her come into the world naturally. Ugh!*

She arrives at 10:44 a.m. I am better prepared for birth the second time around, unafraid and more willing to trust my body. Francesca is delivered on the heels of one massive contraction. My doctor, scrambling to put on his gloves, walks into the room and exclaims, "Woah, woah, Meighan! Slow down."

I laugh out loud. "It's all her," I say proudly. "My daughter."

Frankie moves so fast she bruises her temples on both sides of her head—a natal signature that will have her demanding her life her way.

I tell my husband, "Don't let her out of your sight," as the nurse carries Frankie from my arms. I sense distraction. I'm not as tired as I was after Sebastian's birth, so my radar is unimpaired.

"Did you hear me?" I ask, sensing his unavailability.

He tells me he is preoccupied with the new job. He has a lot to figure out. He gives me a tiny kiss on my forehead, and disbelief washes over me. My silence follows him out of the hospital room. *Abandoned.* I choke on the sour taste creeping up my throat.

I got this, I think.

Sitting upright, I move my legs to the floor. It took me forever to heal after the birth of my son, and a small part of me is afraid to stand up. But everything moves okay. I am surprised at how good I physically feel. I follow my daughter out of the room and watch as they take her first photo. Next is the blood test with a prick of her heel.

Mentally I am at war over my husband's quick exit. *He doesn't want to be here.*

"Deception" by Grandma Margaret

Strange that a shape of face, a glancing eye,
Does not reflect what contours of the mind,
What passions, or serenities, of soul,
Are caught within.
Picasso did not image all his genius.
And you who stand at an impressive size,
With manly mieux, and lengthy vigorous stride,
Are dwarfed inside.

CHAPTER 8

DENIAL

(Don't Even kNow I Am Lying)

I am married to a man who triggers my helplessness.

Resigned to thinking there is nothing I can do, I continue to follow his lead. We spend the next four years moving as he continues to change jobs.

Lansing holds us for ten months. I ask him to secure a one-level home with a fenced yard. Sebastian likes to explore; his fearlessness fuels his daring nature. He is a boy unafraid of the unknown. Our new three-level house is filled with stairs and no gates outside, and we live across the street from a gigantic park.

I join a mom's group that meets three times a week. My goal is to make new friends while raising competent children. I learn about attachment parenting, introducing me to the importance of bonding with my children to promote their confidence. Supporting their independence in specific ways will deliver them a strong sense of security.

We move back to California in time to celebrate Frankie's first birthday. I find a fantastic one-level, three-bedroom apartment in San Rafael with a hot tub. Frankie's favorite place is under water. She loves to submerge herself for what seems like a full minute and pop up, beaming with excitement. Her happiness is thrilling to me. I am mesmerized by her joy.

Sacramento, a few hours north, is our next adventure. I work as a yoga instructor only five minutes from our house, and we rent a wonderful one-level home with two living rooms and a gigantic fenced backyard. We plant vegetables and hang swings from the trees. Frankie and Sebastian now go to preschool together, and I take great pride in making their lunches every day, bold with color and flavor. Their empty lunchboxes are a tremendous motivator until I learn the truth. "We throw it out, Mommy," Sebastian says. "So we bring it home clean," explains Frankie.

After a few months, my husband quits his job. He doesn't like what he's learning, nor does he get along with his colleagues. He finds a new position with a company in San Francisco. The two-hour commute prompts him to rent a room during the week and travel home on weekends. I am grateful to have him gone, but it also needles my dream of a loving family.

Ours is a marriage of inconvenience. We do not get along and we're not friends. Our frustration with each other is only exacerbated by the distance. Weekends are challenging. In his mind, his five-day work week deserves a break. In mine, being with kids for multiple days on end warrants time alone. Our unhappiness is a problem we do not know how to solve, so we blame each other. Our expectations are smoldering embers, always burning.

After teaching my Saturday morning yoga class, I plan to run errands. But I stop home earlier than expected because I've had a strange feeling. When I pull into the garage, my stomach grips. I tried calling earlier to check in, but he didn't answer.

His car is gone. I think, *Where'd they go?* When I open the door, I find our kids alone, playing in the living room. I walk slowly and do my best to stay calm even though I want to erupt. I sit on the couch and ask the kids, "Where's Daddy?"

Sebastian looks up at me, his eyes wide, sensing my irritation. "Daddy's at the store. He told us to be good," he says.

My head feels as if it's in a vise. Pressure grows on the sides as I watch my son place train tracks in a wide circle. Frankie is gathering toy animals to fill the middle area. I sit in silent admiration of their innocence.

My anger burns, slow and steady, a fire preparing to blaze. *Who leaves their children alone?* I move into the kitchen and set about cleaning while I attempt to arrange my thoughts. I have nowhere to go with this awful moment. Who could I possibly tell? It feels insane.

When he opens the door, I start, "What were you thinking?" He moves to the living room and gives the kids their candy. Their happiness hurts.

He turns to me and answers my question in a measured tone. "Meighan, I went to the store. I didn't want to take the kids." His voice doesn't sound sorry or embarrassed, not even upset at being caught. He seems justified. *Oh.*

I can't stop. My voice is loud and clear. "They are three and four years old, too young to stay at home alone. Again, what were you thinking? What if something happened to you? Them?" My feet are firmly planted as I hold on to my hips, giving my hands something to do.

He stands there, watching me spin out. Sebastian and Frankie come into the kitchen. I continue yelling, "I can't believe you would be this selfish! For what? Beer and cigarettes? I am so disgusted! What kind of father does that?" *Who raised you?*

I pause to look at my kids staring up at me.

His silent retreat to the garden only sparks my rage. I watch my husband of six years respond to my verbal attack by disengaging. He takes his brown paper bag out to the patio and lets the door slam shut behind him. Tears erupt, and I slide down the fridge until the linoleum catches me. My kids climb onto my lap, each taking a knee and wrapping their little arms around my body so they can hug me from all sides. They are my tripod.

I consider leaving him for a split second. *Where would I go?* I cannot see beyond what is here. I have no relationship with my own possibility. *What's wrong with me? Why is this so hard?*

Feeling deficient is a vicious motivator. It feeds on hatred and loathing, a silent attacker gnawing at my self-esteem.

Pretending to be happy is exhausting. We buy a house to secure our future. That's what I do—keep adding on in some blind hope I will finally get it right.

It is not my dream home, but it is considered by my husband to be a wise investment. The school district alone encourages me to dismiss my aspirations of a one-level house and a beautiful garden. Little by little I begin to disappear. I willingly stand in my husband's shadow and complain. Misery runs deep through my veins, and I am unable to see my life is a lie.

Mental anxiety and stress have me constantly on the move. I am scheduled to the minute and keep myself super busy. I know how to get things done; my specialty is taking on responsibilities that aren't mine. This is how I hide my brokenness.

Being driven to prove myself is a full-time job. I go to bed every night exhausted, and I wake up stressed each morning. Oblivious to the cycle of abuse I am instilling upon myself, I continue. Stuck in a colorless world without intimacy, I lose my ability to wonder.

In my desperation, I seek out a shaman. I've always been fascinated with ancient healing traditions. Thanks to Google, I find a shaman only twenty minutes away and make an appointment. I carry with me an idea that I need to be fixed. This is the only expectation I have. I work with him for three months. In our second session we discover my root chakra is blocked.

"Meighan?" he asks, with his hands hovering over my body. "Have you ever been sexually assaulted?"

My eyes are closed. "No," I answer immediately as tears fill my eyes and slip down my cheeks. My whole body begins to shake. "Wait. Maybe." *Oh my god.* My weeping continues as I release myself into a new telling of something that happened long ago.

"Untitled" by Grandma Margaret

I want a plain pine box,
Unvarnished, and smelling of the forest.
Or a thimble full of ashes
(can more than fifty years
be so reduced, so trivial?)
Scattered from a high hill.
I want no pennies on my eyes,
but flowers, flowers;
for the smell of death is bad I hear,
and lilacs would supplant it.
No one needs to look at me,
for I shall not look back.
There will be just silence;
Sunshine, warm and sweet in the still air,
And the slow curve of time,
returning to me,
like a memory.

CHAPTER 9

TAKEN (MEMORY)

On my eighteenth birthday, a few months after my dad's death, I sneak out to go to a New Year's Eve party with friends. Mom told me not to go. I didn't listen.

I drink too much alcohol. I want to be like the popular kids, cool and daring.

Preoccupied with a dark-haired boy, my eyes follow him around the house. He flirts with the girls surrounding him, and I spend most of my time eavesdropping on his conversations. He doesn't know I'm alive. Losing myself to imagination, I wonder what my life would be like if he noticed me, if he were my boyfriend, if we were together.

As we step into 1985, I think about Dad, and anger surfaces. He's been dead for two months. I walk outside to feel the night air on my face. I move my eyes toward the heavens to whisper, "Bye, Dad! Fuck you for leaving me!"

Some of the stars merge with the moon. My vision is affected by all the beer I've been drinking. In my dizziness, I head back inside to find people everywhere. Some are passed out. Some are getting their eyebrows shaved off. Bedroom doors are locked while lovers play, and others are talking.

I see my friend standing not too far away. I think she is looking at me, but I'm not totally sure. I walk closer. "Let's hit it so we can get up early tomorrow?" she says.

These words make me happy because I really don't want to drink another beer. "Great idea," I slur.

We set up the pull-out in the middle of the living room. I slip off my shoes, and we crawl under the covers fully clothed.

I curl up near the edge, facing the wall and close my eyes. *How can I be dizzy while lying down?*

Someone is pulling at my arms while I am being elbowed and shushed by my friend behind me. Confused and irritated, I'm not sure what I'm supposed to do. I open one eye to find the cute popular guy coaxing me out of bed. He wants my attention. "Meighan," I hear. "Get up. Let's hang out."

"Huh?" I mumble.

He says it again, "C'mon, Meighan."

I try to move. It's not easy. I stand up. He wraps his arms around me.

"I've been watching you all night. Don't go to bed yet. It's too early," he whispers.

Really? I think. *It's like way past 2:00 a.m.*

"Meighan," he says, smiling. "Come over here. Finally, I get to have you all to myself." He hands me a beer and motions me toward a mattress on the floor.

He wants me? How does he know my name? How does he know how to pronounce it? My mom says my Grandpa Grant, on my dad's side, found the spelling and the pronunciation for my name. The "gh" is silent, making it sound like "me-in." *Nobody ever gets it right. It always involves a conversation.*

He starts kissing me. My curiosity has me exploring gently, but his lips are tight and his tongue is tense. *I don't like it.* The discomfort makes me cold, and my body gets stiff. Bleary-eyed with fatigue and drunkenness, I am not completely aware of what is happening. My clothes are being peeled off me, and I can't seem to prevent it.

"Uh, what are we doing?" I ask uncomfortably.

He kisses me again. He's doing all the moving, pushing my legs apart. I don't think it is a good idea. I slowly go still. In my head I'm thinking this must mean something.

Then I say, "No, this isn't what I want to do." He puts his lips on mine to hush my words. I refuse to take off my tights and keep them around my ankles. *I don't want to lose them.*

"Ouch. That hurts," I whimper. I've never had sex before. I only imagined what it might feel like from the old movies I watch. Long slow kisses, sensual smiles, and romantic whispering—desire looks beautiful to me on screen. This feels horrible, empty, without tenderness. It has a forced quality I don't understand.

"It's okay. Everything will be okay." *No. No. No. No. No.*

Holding on to my thoughts seems like the only way I can get through it. *He wants me... He needs me.*

Someone flips on the lights. In my nakedness I move my hands to cover my face. I peer through the spaces between my fingers to see too many eyes looking down at me. Humiliation burns through my body. I can't move. I don't know what to do. I hear laughing.

I don't belong to me. I am yours for the taking.

"Untitled" by Grandma Margaret

The language of the land is old
And speaks the gnarled truth of time;
From lair, and nest, and budding tree,
In liquid syllables of rain.
Ancient calligraphy of roots,
Of deep and convoluted trails
Where rivers run; I see your songs,
Grooved in the trembling core of earth,
And carved in granite on the plain.

CHAPTER 10

PIZZA

Movies have been my medicine ever since I was old enough to enjoy them. I am easily obsessed with old musicals and love stories. When the shaman suggests I watch videos to promote my healing, I am surprised. *No way.* He recommends young romances like *Pretty in Pink* and *The Breakfast Club* to assist me in reimagining my "first time." He gives me permission to change my story.

He recommends another film and tells me I need to receive a message, something important. His lack of detail has me curiously irritated. *Why can't he just tell me?* "Watch *Free Willy* with your kids. Your spirit animal orca has something for you to know," he says before our session ends.

Overwhelmed with the fact that I never viewed my first sexual experience as a rape, I look at all the years between then and now. The difference between having sex and making love is not something I understand. Trusting my body and sharing it with another, generously and playfully, is an expression of intimacy I have not yet experienced. I think back to that awful night on my eighteenth birthday and the thought I carried home: *Is this what everyone wants?* I didn't enjoy sex then or after. I used it to get attention. It became something else for me to do. *How messed up am I?*

I have difficulty believing the shaman's remedy. It seems too simple, silly even. I put it aside for now and pick up *Free Willy* from the video store before I head home to make popcorn.

Sebastian's gray eyes find mine, and we share a wink. Just this morning I found him in the kitchen trying to make me breakfast.

"I wanted to surprise you, Mom," he says.

"You did? What's the plan?" I ask looking around at his tremendous effort.

"I was thinking scrambled eggs, potatoes, bagels, and fruit. But I don't really know how to cook, so now I'm hoping cereal will make you happy."

I laugh as I wrap my arms around him and say, "That's all I feel like eating right now." His relief is obvious as we set up a bowl for his sister.

Frankie is busy coloring and wearing heart-shaped sunglasses indoors. Her white-blond hair is pulled in two pigtails and makes her appear more playful than usual. Looking at her is like swallowing a rainbow.

Here is a girl who likes to push her own limits. Yesterday she committed herself to swimming underwater from one end of the community pool to the next. Every time she had to stop for a breath, she'd blind me with her smile and move to start again.

With the popcorn ready, I add butter and parmesan cheese, something I've done since I was a teen. The story involves a troubled young boy, Jesse, who ends up doing community service at a theme park where he bonds with Willy, the orca whale in captivity. All three of us are fully invested, eager to know what happens. Keenly awaiting my message, I can't believe what I hear when it arrives.

I rewind the film to watch it again. There it is, clear as day, a moment where Willy needs to jump over the breakwater to get to his family on the other side: Don't be afraid to set yourself free.

I am completely dumbfounded. *Free from what? Pain? Unhappiness?*

My last session with the shaman is a whirlwind. He opens the door to let me in, and I start talking. "What does *setting myself free* mean exactly? Free from what? Am I supposed to know?" I ask impatiently, moving to sit down in my usual spot.

The minute those last words leave my mouth I realize the answer must be yes. I most likely need to dig deep and figure out for myself what it means, which just makes me mad. *How the hell do I do that?*

He takes the seat across from me and smiles gently. Frustrated by his calm demeanor, I wonder if he appreciates my upside down. The silence pinches me, and I think I need to repeat myself.

He meets my questions with one of his own. *Typical.*

"Let me ask you something," he starts. "Why do you want to stay married to someone who is afraid of you?"

He sits back and quietly meets my waiting. I suppose he's giving me time to consider. I can't. I am speechless, dumbfounded. My weeping is unexpected. His question terrifies me and rips me apart inside. So much so that I refuse to believe it. I just can't. *How could I be married to someone who is afraid of me?* This is impossible for me to digest. I wrap his question tightly and slip it beside the list of romance movies I plan to watch someday.

Unable to imagine my life without my husband, I stay.

The drinking in our home escalates. We spent hours every night consuming bottles of wine and smoking multiple packs of cigarettes. Our addictions feed our unhappiness. One night I tell him, "I can't do this anymore. While we are out here complaining, television is raising our children. This isn't the mom I want to be."

I quit smoking and stop drinking. Without these two elements in my life, I presume everything will improve.

My life keeps spiraling. I hide bottles and empty bottles. I am nasty. I feel justified. I'm mean. I yell. I let my misery take over. I am haunted by what is not here. His silence shows me I am invisible. All this chaos mirrors my childhood, the feelings are the same, and I cannot connect the dots.

The emotional tension is impossible to describe. I am furious with the world. My marriage is meaningless. I am angry and full of blame. *I am terrified of losing all I have gained.* And this is the biggest lie of all.

We continue like this for two more years.

My husband's eventual unemployment lands him drinking on the couch and watching TV all day. I start working with my family in San Francisco to help with the bills. He stops functioning altogether and repeatedly forgets to pick up the kids after school. Concerned parents call me daily, and I cringe with embarrassment.

I decide we need a dog, hoping the responsibility will cure my husband's depression. We find Vespa at the pound, a black lab mix. Her presence saves us emotionally, at least for me and the kids. My husband's disinterest has her in the cage when he's at home.

"How long has she been in there?" I say to him one evening.

"Why don't you ask her?" he says.

Dumbfounded, I let Vespa out.

Our marriage hangs limply between us. We sleep in separate bedrooms and become absolute strangers.

Al-Anon, a recovery system for loved ones of alcoholics, gives me hope. Daily meetings provide unconditional support. I dive into new pools for healing. I work the program at my own pace, and on Saturday mornings, my children attend Alakid. Faith-based wisdom introduces us to twelve steps, a higher power, and a community.

Initially thinking my husband is my qualifier, I sink into my seat one day at a meeting and remember my dad. *Oh. He was my first alcoholic.* The confusion and the pain that surround me at home are so familiar. I cry and explain and repeat often in meetings how my husband's behavior, his choices, his neglect, his *everything* is my problem. I am convinced that by being in these rooms I will learn how to get him to stop drinking.

Turning the focus inward is unfamiliar. I've never done it. Working with my sponsor, someone who guides me through the twelve steps and becomes a trusted friend, shows me the value of a healthy relationship. It blows me away as it is unlike anything I've ever experienced. I find courage to change and to understand, fundamentally, that I can only control myself if I am willing.

Standing up in a room filled with over one hundred people, I find the words, "I thought I was here to cure my husband, and realize now I am here because of my dad, to heal myself." *I've been holding on for a lifetime.* This realization makes me lighter for the first time in a long while.

As I drive home from the meeting, relief fills me. Acknowledging and sharing my secrets is a big step in a new direction.

Walking through the front door, my husband stands in front of me, smiling. My surprise is enhanced when I see he is about to say something. I smile back, encouraged.

He announces unabashedly, "I want a divorce."

My mouth falls open. He turns and walks out the front door and adds, "The kids are hungry." I hear him get in his car and drive away.

Stranded in the foyer, I holler to my kids, "Who wants pizza?"

"Mitigation" by Grandma Margaret

Fog
Muffles the trees' sharp blackness;
Hangs a pale ruffle
across the hills.
Fog mutes the sea's voice;
Filters the light
to lavender and pearl.
Can it thus alter,
That stark innominate
landscape of the mind?
Blur its edges,
Damp its arid wastes?
Fog
lies on my face,
like rain or tears.
I swallow carefully,
Lest it choke me.

CHAPTER 11

KNOWING

Who will I be without my marriage?

I am nothing, nobody, paralyzed. Post-divorce is gruesome.
Fear keeps me from imagining possibility. I believe I've
failed everyone—my kids, my husband, my family, even me.
I've reduced myself to barely functioning in public. My hiding continues. In private, I stay quiet to gather my strength.

*Who am I in this new place of losing what I worked so hard
to create?* What's difficult for me to admit is that it was a
life I didn't like. On the outside it looked pretty, maybe even
ideal. But on the inside, it was torture.

Ten years of reacting describes who I've been. It is proof I
did not know myself. If I see what is here, I get a sliver of
knowing. I'm at that place where I need to stand strong and
make a choice.

But I don't know what to do with myself when I'm alone
without my kids. It seems wrong and unnatural and pathetic.
I'm smart enough to know I've been using my kids and my

role as their mother to *not* look at myself. I'm slow to hold the truth of my part in my marriage and my unhappiness. I've been blaming others for a lifetime. It's hard for me to live with the pain of loss. I don't like it.

But I'm also learning that it is okay to talk about what hurts.

I lie on my bed for hours, staring at the ceiling while my head dances around the room, losing time. My home is clean, organized, and photo ready. Vespa came with me after the divorce. We walk in the early mornings. I pray to the stars for hope as moonshine lights my path and reminds me of magic.

When I'm with my kids everything makes sense. My purpose is clear. Missing them is a suffering unlike any other.

My emotions get the better of me while driving Sebastian and Frankie to their dad's. I can't stop crying. The more I try, the worse it gets. My kids beg me to tell them what's wrong, and I don't know how to explain it.

They hate my silence.

"Mom," Sebastian says. "Maybe if you tell us we can help." I look at him in the rearview mirror, sitting upright in his booster seat and imploring me with his gray eyes. I am reminded of the day he ran home from being in the woods for hours, demanding my full attention. He tells me to follow him, so I can see the fairy house he and his sister built. He's always been great at helping me see what's most important.

"Yeah, Mom," Frankie adds. "You always say to let it out. Then we can deal with it together." She's buckled into her car seat. I turn my head and see her shrug her shoulders in a "what gives?" gesture.

It's the same look she gave a few days ago, standing in the doorway covered in poop. She'd spent the afternoon following deer in the woods, staying low to the ground so as not to be seen. I laughed so hard with delight and pride. *My daughter is amazing.* She tells me everything as I wash her off, and we relive every single detail of her adventure. She, too, has a talent for showing me what matters most.

Here are two of my favorite people asking me to come clean. Burden keeps me from talking. I don't want to barf my troubles onto their shoulders. Stopped at a red light, I let them know the truth.

"I don't want to share you," I say, unleashing a moan so deep I startle myself.

This open selfishness feels strange. What does it mean? Is it okay? How can my children possibly understand? The difficulty I have with their dad is not their problem, but they suffer from it. Will we ever find ourselves as parents, or will we always be on opposite sides?

"How long will we be with Dad?" Frankie asks innocently.

"Just the weekend. I will pick you up from school on Monday," I answer, inhaling slowly and gripping the steering wheel tightly. My clenched fingers restrict blood flow.

"Mom," Sebastian starts. "We'll talk every night. I promise."

I don't have the heart to remind him of his dad's no-cell-phone policy.

We had such a silly time when the three of us sat on the floor of the Verizon store for hours. I unsuccessfully taught them how to text on flip phones. We exchanged the devices for smartphones before we left the store. Hoodwinked by my eight-year-old son and seven-year-old daughter, I surmise on our car ride home—amid squeals of delight—that they were born too late, clearly a generation wired for new and updated versions of everything.

"Of course, Sebastian," I backpedal. "Can't wait."

I drop them at his house and watch them run down the drive-way. I've never been inside, nor have I met his fiancée. "Stay out," reads the invisible sign above the door. He refuses to have me meet the soon-to-be stepmother of our children; he tells me it will never happen. I spoke with him a few weeks ago in this very spot, hoping to shift us into a new way of relating with each other, suggesting the three adults come together to coparent. His smiling and congenial demeanor felt condescending. I sensed it when he laughed at my suggestion. And then I realized something bizarre. He likes it this way. He needs me to be wrong so he can have someone to hate.

While married, my husband's absence and presence continuously stoked my anger. My self-hatred was the problem, but I couldn't see it. I questioned my role as a wife because our marriage was so far from anything I'd ever imagined. I was a silent partner. *No. Less than that.* I was just a miserable person faking my way through. Secretly, it felt like I was carrying around a bowling ball that behaved like a black hole, constantly being reminded of what wasn't here.

What is this new place for us? It is separated and undefined, and it feels worse. Maybe it is exactly what I need.

I think of my kids. *Trust them.* They know what they are doing.

Last year, squished into a student chair, I waited for Frankie's teacher. I looked around at the hanging artwork to see if I recognized my daughter's pieces. I played this game with myself every time I entered one of my kids' classrooms. *Will I know them?*

Her teacher walked in with long, wavy, brown hair that accentuated the pale blue of her blouse hanging loosely above dark jeans and beige flats. She was Sebastian's kindergarten teacher too, so we were familiar.

"Hi, Meighan," she said as she sat down. "It's nice to see you again." I smiled until I heard her next sentence, which shifted my face into a look of confusion.

Across from me, she leaned in to ask, as if in secret, "Is Frankie a girl or a boy?" This is how my second kindergarten parent/teacher conference began. My first one, the previous year, was focused quite specifically on why my son couldn't rhyme. I spent twenty minutes defending my kids' disinterest in Dr. Seuss books. What I was slow to understand was how rhyming helps children develop important literacy skills for brain development. Once I was able to get past feeling like a lousy parent, I ran to the bookstore.

"What?" I said, trying to sit more comfortably in my chair. *She's a girl,* I thought. Maybe I was wrong. Then another thought bubbled up.

A few months earlier, Frankie had buzzcut her hair. Raquel, our friend, did the honors. I wanted no part in the massacre. I considered destroying her lovely long blond locks a form of sacrilege. I relented because I possessed an even stronger desire for my daughter to have a say, for her to know she has a right to explore and choose how she presents herself to the world.

I can see already at the age of five that Frankie has a strong vision. She knows what she wants, is eager and unafraid. Fearless. She possesses no doubt.

Frankie currently prefers wearing her brother's clothes. She likes them for a boatload of reasons. "They're comfy...they're cool...they're my brother's," she tells me again and again. Long gone are the floral patterns and the frills and the dresses of her pre-K days.

Today, she looks like a boy, and I don't see the problem. I prefer to support her uniqueness. It's fun and easy, and it feels important. I did not possess such bravery when I was her age.

So was not prepared for this conversation with her teacher, mainly because I didn't anticipate it. I was ready to tackle academic processing and social behavior. *Does she know her alphabet yet? Can Frankie rhyme?* These thoughts floated around my head.

Frankie's teacher continued, "Frankie is confusing…to the other kids." As if this was supposed to make me care. She looked at me with concern in her eyes, and it put me off.

I paused for effect. I didn't really know what to say. Then I sat up a little taller and blurted out, "Did you ask her?"

"No," she replied. "I thought I would speak with you first." She appeared unhappy with my response, like she was hoping for something different.

"Honestly," I admitted, "I've not had this discussion with Frankie. I know her to be a girl who likes to wear her brother's clothes. I will of course speak with her today. But if you need guidance, getting it from her is my recommendation. Maybe ask her in the morning, before class starts, to let her decide each day?" I said it with pride. This felt reasonable.

The twenty-five minutes was gobbled up with Frankie's gender identity, so we didn't discuss anything else. I drove home wondering how I might pursue this conversation with my daughter. *Is it important? Frankie needs to be comfortable in her own skin. I can give her the space to decide for herself. I want to support her knowing.*

Watching my children operate from a confident place makes me not want to stand in their way or impede their growth. I found my answer. If I can support Sebastian and Frankie's intuition and love them as they are, maybe I can do the same for myself. If the direction is not clear, I will pause and wait for clarity. *Yes, trust my knowing. It will surface when it is ready.*

"To A New Moon" by Grandma Margaret

Bleak and cratered planet,
Vast mountainous and desert world,
Where man and his machines have visited;
Can this be you?
Translucent in the evening sky,
Balancing your pale and fragile crescent,
Against the on rushing dark.

CHAPTER 12

DAHLIAS

I resign myself to never having sex again.

The stress of change takes a toll. I do not feel attractive, let alone desirable. With the end of my marriage, the prospect of intimacy is daunting. The thought of being naked with another is terrifying, absolutely impossible. Nope, not for me.

I do my best to move beyond paralysis without my kids. I fill my days working at our family restaurant, attending Al-Anon meetings, teaching or practicing yoga, and artmaking.

After meditating and journaling this morning, I gaze through the French doors to my garden and envision plants to provide a splash of living color. I phone a flower shop nearby.

"Flowers Above and Beyond," says the voice on the other end of the line. "Shaffer speaking."

"Hi," I say, "I want to create a living expression of color on my deck."

"Yes," I hear. "How may I help you?"

Something about this voice draws me in, a strong resonance soft around the edges, firm and inviting. I'm a little distracted by it and lose my train of thought for a second. A part of me wants to keep listening and doesn't understand why he's stopped talking.

"I'm not completely sure," I say, feeling silly as I attempt to regroup. "I think I'm asking for a consultation. Is that something you offer?"

"Absolutely," he says kindly. "When would you like to come by?"

"I can be there in a few hours. Will that work?" I ask hopefully.

"Yes," he says, and I smile with relief. "What's your name?"

"My name is Meighan," I answer.

I meet Shaffer, the owner of the flower shop, in the early afternoon to discuss my ideas. He is tall and handsome in a rustic sort of way. I like his work boots, jeans, and plaid shirt. They are unassuming and give the impression he is not afraid to work hard. He has a full head of brown, curly hair peppered with some gray that looks soft around his full face. Shaffer is a big guy.

With genuine interest in my project, he asks detailed questions like, "How large is your deck?" "What is the height of your railing?" and "What are you hoping to create?" Unprepared, I answer to the best of my ability.

"Do you have a flower in mind?" he asks.

"Dahlias," I say.

"They represent beauty..." He looks at me, and I feel the blood rush to my face. "...commitment and kindness," he finishes.

Yes, I think, *that will do nicely.* I look down at the ruby reds and deep purples of the dahlias in front of me and imagine their richness sitting in tall pots at the edge of my deck.

"I suspect I'll need nine plants total," I tell Shaffer, pointing to the colors I want, "and three of those tall clay pots over there." They are a faded pink-beige color, which will enhance the saturation of the flowers. He loads everything into the back of my car as we make small talk, and I consider purchasing something else just to stay near him. *Does he feel it too?*

"Meighan," he says, and I turn to look up into his hazel eyes. "Please take my number and call me if you ever need a hand with anything." My fingers lightly brush his as I move to take the card, sending an electric current up my arm. *Is this really happening?*

We start texting each other short messages of hellos and happenings in our lives, which quickly turns into long conversations over the phone. I am unused to having this feeling, this desire to talk with another and receive his attention happily. I don't question any of it. I just enjoy what we create together. I presume he is married, so I label us "friends." I stop by his shop often to purchase flowers and recognize I am a different person when I am around him.

Soon, we talk every morning on his drive to work. If my kids are home and asleep, I go outside to walk Vespa so I won't wake them with my laughter. I look up at the stars to tell Shaffer what I see, and we share our knowledge of constellations. This early time of day is precious to me. The quiet in the night before it turns light is a silent prayer for my imagination.

Shaffer tells me he likes the sound of my voice and the way I think. His attention makes me lighthearted and playful—a welcome respite from the heavy drama of my life. The crisp morning air is a seedling of innocence inspiring possibility.

Whatever we are cultivating has us acting like teenagers. We are giddy, absorbed, and eager to connect. Sometimes we talk about it, but mostly we just enjoy it. This morning Shaffer is frustrated with an employee and anticipates her calling in sick, giving him more work to do.

"Well," I say, "if she doesn't want to work, maybe it's better she's not there?"

"You're too young to understand," he teases.

"Hey, now," I say. "Since when is forty-nine young?"

"Who's forty-nine? You can't be older than thirty-five," Shaffer says sincerely. I don't know what to say here. Could he really think I was that young—an age before I had children?

"Meighan," he continues, "what do you think this is between us?" *Uh oh*, I think. *Here we go.*

"A friendship?" I question apprehensively. Whatever *this* is, I don't want it to end. Getting plucked off my cloud would be unsettling.

"Really?" he asks. "That's what you think this is?"

Now I feel a little stupid. I'm not sure what I am supposed to say and, honestly, have no idea what we are doing. All I know is I like it, and I don't want it to stop.

I swallow my fear. "Shaffer, are you married?"

"No." He laughs.

"Oh," I say, stumped. "I thought maybe you were married. I mean, why wouldn't you be?"

"I was, once," he says. "Not anymore. And Meighan, how could you think I was married when I spend all this time getting to know you?"

I think about this while my heartbeat quickens. It's so uncomfortable to sit with the truth of believing I am unattractive or not worth anyone's time. But that's what had me thinking he was married. I feel foolish and ridiculously naive. My face is beet red with embarrassment. I'm glad he can't see me.

"I am very attracted to you, Meighan," he says with confidence. "I am interested in being more than friends. So I would like you to think about that and decide what it means for you."

"Okay," I say softly. I almost add "thank you" and keep my mouth closed.

We plan to meet in the early morning at my home in a few days. He'll stop over on his way to work.

We chat while he drives, and I make coffee. We are both giddy with excitement.

"There will be no kissing and no funny business," he tells me through a smile over the phone. "Be sure to keep your clothes on," he chides. "Turn the lights on bright and don't distract me with your beauty. Make sure you are fully clothed. Layers are preferred. Pull out cards and board games so we have something to do."

"I've prepared food," I say, throwing bagels in the toaster. "Will eating be a reasonable pastime?" Butterflies flutter in my belly. I do my best not to imagine anything and boil water for coffee.

"Yes," he says. "Anything not involving touching will be great."

When he's ten minutes away, the power goes out. "Um, Shaffer," I say, trying to hold back from laughter. "I have something I need to tell you."

"Yes, dear?" he welcomes.

"I've just lost power, and I do not own any candles," I say seriously, secretly thrilled with the possibilities.

"Young lady," he says, "you have got to be kidding me." I love the sound of his voice and the way he makes me feel young and appreciated.

I lean against the door and wait. I hear his truck pull up and step outside to greet him. The darkness of the morning is mysterious and makes whatever we are doing seem secret. He walks slowly up the driveway while my heart beats louder with anticipation and my face hurts from smiling. His presence alone lifts my feet off the ground so I am floating. He steps forward as I walk backward. We move together, and when he crosses my threshold, I close the door so we stand in the dark facing each other.

"Welcome," I whisper.

"Shh," he says softly. I place my hand on his chest and feel his breath warming the space between us.

His lips find mine, and I am carried away on a cloud of pixie dust. His tongue is gentle and smooth, delicately inviting me closer. Unfamiliar with the magnificent desire brewing within, I find myself in complete surrender.

Flames of passion course through me like none I've ever felt before. Shaffer plants kisses along my neck and shoulders, each nibble an electric pulse, like shooting stars from the heavens. I am overwhelmed with sensation and amazed by my body's response to his touch. We kiss, lost in each other's embrace for what feels like a timeless moment.

Shaffer pulls back. "No more," he says breathlessly. "This is where we stop. You need some candles, woman."

Dizzy with excitement, I don't want to stop, but I appreciate the chance to savor what just happened. Shaffer is true to himself in every way and has a strong moral code. He is the first man to show me the respect I deserve and have yet to exhibit toward myself. We hold hands, drink coffee, and talk until the sun rises before he leaves for work. His slow pace challenges my urgent patterning, and I experience firsthand the beauty of sensuality in all its expressions.

Shaffer sleeps over on the nights my kids are with their dad. He never wants my children to think I am unavailable to them.

Entwined in each other's arms, something new for both of us, we lose ourselves deep in sleep and fall hard. It occurs to me I've never felt safe with another human being. I hear the tweeting of birds meandering through the living room to gently pull me awake. I settle into his arms around me and barely whisper, "What just happened? My body feels so heavy."

"I have a theory about that," he says, nibbling my ear. He understands me. His response is immediate. We are connected. "When we sleep, our souls leave our bodies. That's why we experience that intense stillness, like we're dead weight."

"Yes." I smile. "That's exactly it. Where do our souls go?" I ask.

"They travel to the heavens and dance together among the stars," he says confidently. I kiss him slow and long as I believe what he says to be true.

We find the time to go on dates, to make love for hours, to catch up on much-needed sleep. Our ability to bend toward each other and around our responsibilities is such a wonderful experience. As we say yes to each other, we find more room to be together. We look for reasons to connect outside of our morning ritual, and we find countless opportunities to meet up for coffee, a walk in the park, a quick trip to Ikea, school functions. Nothing seems to be off limits for us. This type of involvement carries great meaning for me as it was not present in my marriage. Shaffer's entire being and the way he relates with me and my kids is something I thought only existed in fairytales.

I tell him everything about my past, including the boy who took something from me without permission. I speak with Shaffer about my shamanic homework, and we watch young love movies together because he wants to support my reimagining.

With him I move beyond the awful experience of my past. He is gentle and patient with my unfolding. When I am unsure, maybe shy because I feel unpracticed, he lovingly says, "Meighan, trust your body. It knows."

I used to think if I was honest about what scared me it would push others away, presenting me as broken or flawed. Until now, I never understood how much harm I was causing. Hiding hurts. Shaffer welcomes my past without judgment.

"Knowing you fully, Meighan," he whispers into my ear one night, "is a precious gift. It may not be possible, but I am very interested in trying." His ability to hold all of me shows the value of acceptance in a loving way.

Our relationship lasts one year. Shaffer sells his business and chooses a life that does not involve a commute. I struggle with his absence for a while. Letting go does not come easy. Explaining it to my children is another hurdle of immense proportions. And we get through it. I explain we are so lucky to know men like Shaffer exist in the world and how his patience, understanding, humor, and kindness are important qualities we can all aim to exhibit.

Shaffer showed me nothing is silly about reimagining my past. He stands as my first teenage love. We created a sensually rich romance filled with pleasure that will serve me forever. My innocence was guided forward through pure desire. He reflected what I couldn't acknowledge before we met—my deep capacity for love.

"A Painting for the Living Room"
by Grandma Margaret

Passion on a wall
is not appropriate.
These mauve and purple wings
webbed with pulsing veins of ink,
seem sacrilege in suburbia.
Emerald fringes to turquoise;
and my lawn, too,
melts toward the sky
on this luminous night.
But the painting bleeds across the room,
And I run to wipe up all those dreams.

CHAPTER 13

NITS

Our custody arrangement adjusts every few months, preventing me and my kids from settling into a routine. Anguish moves in, keeping my nervous system in survival mode.

"Court ordered" becomes only words on paper. I have no control. When our kids are with their dad, anything goes. Pick-up and drop-off times are disregarded. Kid phones are not allowed and contact with Mom is not supported. For three months, my kids bring lice weekly into our home. The sheets and pajamas I send to his house are returned, unopened. Frankie tells me her dad doesn't want my help.

We ritualize the combing of nits after every pick-up from Dad's house. In the beginning, I am angry and irritated with the two-hour inconvenience, but this detail of infestation is impossible for me to accept, and the demand for me to fix it feels too big.

Pillows on the floor hold my children, and towels drape over their shoulders like warm blankets. I massage their hair while hiding my disgust of the situation. *This is my life.* A part of me doesn't want to see the bugs or to admit they are here. Everything changes when I commit myself to the truth.

After a few weeks, we settle into the beauty of ceremony. As absurd as it sounds, we start to relax together. My children at ease is a beautiful sight. Frankie gets so still when I work the comb through her hair. Sebastian too. Sometimes he lets his eyes close. *A mother's care, my hands, loving them… here we are.*

We sit in the living room with snacks, TV, and Vamousse, the best lice treatment around. It foams up white and the black nits appear, so we can see them. We share the triumph together. It's ridiculous, and it's ours.

Through surrender, I find an expression of love.

We struggle with shared custody. I don't know why it is so hard, but the transition between households is dramatic and emotional. My kids call me every week, desperate and unhappy. It turns me upside down.

"Please, Mom, come get me. I don't want to be here," Frankie cries one night.

"Dad locked us in our rooms so we can't see each other," Sebastian explains.

My helplessness is suffocating, and I cry as the words leave my mouth. "My hands are tied," I tell them both. "I can't do anything." I sound like a broken record, and the cracks in my heart deepen.

Time seems to creep by as we fall into a rhythm of doing less when we are together. I am reluctant to accept this as a good thing. A therapist, recommended by a friend, comes to our home because I am afraid our lack of motivation is a problem.

She visits for three hours. We start in the living room seated in a circle. I am surprised to see my kids so animated. They are excited to speak about everything. I remove myself from the group when the therapist wants to visit with them alone.

Waiting in my garden, I scan the greenery looking for a spot to rest my gaze, I'm nervous and worried. *I need to calm down and trust we will figure this out.* Leaning back in my seat I take a deep breath. I close my eyes to slow my thinking.

She speaks to me as she walks through the slider onto the deck. "Let them do nothing," she says. "They need to unwind after the stress they endure over there. Your house is where they get to decompress."

I have iced tea on a tray in front of us. Picking up her glass, she says, "They are worried about you. They need you to be okay." She takes a sip. "In their world, you are all they have."

Me. Tears pierce my eyes. *They're concerned for me.* Their young hearts and little bodies needing me to be okay. *Of course they do.* The attention is a surprise. *Our care is reciprocal.*

This emboldens me. A feeling of strength rises in my spine, and I sense my power. This marks the day our triad becomes less scheduled. I don't want to *make* us do anything.

"Ambition" by Grandma Margaret

I am too sane to be a poet.
Writing of bread, and bulbs, and children; of
the seasons,
and their attendant changes in the soul.
I know something of love, and disappointment.
I feel attached to nature,
and to that strange yet universal human
who lives in me and in my neighbor.
But would I were mad!
Mad, and unique, and safe,
From the abhorrent anonymity.

CHAPTER 14

EPO

I need to find my dad.

Someone told me years ago he was buried in San Rafael. Heading home from the mall, after a shopping spree for kid clothes, we pass the cemetery. I never saw him dead and don't remember a casket or a burial ceremony. *Why is that?*

For a long time, I didn't believe he died. Since then, I've decided a dead body will provide the closure needed for the bereaved to move on.

I travel three blocks and dramatically step on the breaks, bringing the car to a swift halt, and then make an immediate U-turn in the middle of the street. It's dramatic and bold. *Kind of crazy.* I'm invigorated.

"Mom!" they scream. "What's happening?"

"Aren't we supposed to be going to Dad's house?" Francesca asks.

"Yes, in an hour. We have time. We're going to find *my* dad, today, right now," I say defiantly.

"What?" they ask.

"My dad—your grandpa," I say, loud and clear. I'm claiming something. Empowered is a good flavor in my mouth, nowhere near the sour I've been tasting with divorce and shared custody.

We drive through the gated entrance and park in front of a single building. Walking inside, I approach a podium that holds a directory. Flipping through the pages, scanning for the letter L, my finger trails down the list of names until I find him: Michael Williams Leibert, "resident."

"He's here," I say, above a whisper. "Section C, plot number twenty-seven."

Frankie finds a paper map of the grounds and encouragingly tells me, "Let's go find him, Mom!"

Sebastian suggests we start high and work our way down. I follow his lead and drive the main road to weave through the cemetery twice, completely unsure how best to proceed. On our third time through, we find section C and Sebastian says, "Mom, let's walk. We can't see anything from the car."

We park.

I climb a hill and think, *It's a beautiful day for a desperate adventure.*

Sebastian and Frankie seem excited and are playful in their hunt, which balances out my dark mood. I carry with me a frustration of not knowing where he is, who he is, and why he left me.

The air is ripe with possibility, but I am tangled up inside. Heat from the sun makes me thirsty. *I have water in the car.* I sit down and touch the green grass surrounding me. *Dad, where are you?* I scan the hillside, looking at a community marked with a variety of colors, bright bouquets of love. *Does anybody put flowers on your grave?*

Lost in thought and losing hope, my son's voice pulls me back to the present. "I found him, Mom! He's over here!"

I stand up to see Frankie run toward her brother, bouncing along. I'm the last to arrive. "Good job! This is amazing!" I say to my son.

Sebastian is beaming with pride. I look down at the dark gray stone engraved with Dad's name and see he is next to his parents. *A family, together.*

I am fixated on his date of death, something I did not commit to memory. It bursts me wide open. *Oh my god.* "Dad died on October 29, 1984," I say aloud.

"Mom," I hear my daughter say. "That's my birthday."

"Yes, sweet girl. You were born twenty-three years after he died." *How is that possible?*

My tears are a combination of relief, sadness, and surprise. My son joins me without hesitation. Frankie doesn't quite understand my emotional expression and greets it by dropping her head, hiding a shy smile.

We're here with you, Dad.

All three of us put our hands on the stone and say hi. Then we lie on our backs, with our heads surrounding his name to take a selfie.

We leave the cemetery happy, fulfilled, and connected. Sebastian and Frankie are curious about their grandpa, and I tell them everything I can remember about his theater.

This is exactly the kind of thrill and delight I need. Dropping my kids off with their dad seems easier today. I watch them run down the driveway and smile. I drive home satisfied.

Later when I fall asleep, Dad visits my dreams and I know his love for me is strong.

I wake the next morning ready for an Al-Anon meeting. Connecting my kids with their grandpa gave us a thread to the past we've been missing. And for some reason, I seem less lost, making me eager to tackle some hard stuff.

Seated with over two hundred fellows in the only place I am not self-conscious, I surrender. Being honest and transparent with the pain I carry is welcome here and lovingly encouraged. The comfort I experience comes from the tenderness that lives in these rooms. I do not hide here.

My learning is a gradual process. Shifting my attitude in all my relationships happens slowly. Not caring what my ex-husband does or doesn't do is a huge pill to swallow. Understanding he and my kids each have their own higher powers is another tough nut. When I refuse to give them the dignity to be their own people, I get overwhelmed. And that's on me.

The truth of what I am uncovering is massive. *How could I have been so off base?* I'm told alcoholism is a family disease, and denial affects everyone living in the home. Being the child of an alcoholic caused me a lot of hurt growing up. Insecurity hardwired me to fix, to solve, to prove myself. I developed an inflated sense of purpose early on. I would do anything for anyone because I believed my happiness was predicated on pleasing others.

My screwed-up thinking is the trouble, along with my victim attitude and blame. Happiness is an option I openly resist. *If patterns of behavior are karmic imprints, is my suffering an inherited legacy?* Alone with my grief, I am filled with a love that has nowhere to go.

For so long I believed my parents were responsible for my happiness, I had no idea it was an inside job. Their preoccupation with their own lives was not something I understood. In fact, I remember being irritated by it as a child. As I sit in this room trying to figure out who I am as a divorced mother of two children, I grasp the importance of identity. *Who am I?*

As a child, young adult, and new mom, I never learned to value myself. In Al-Anon, I am given permission and tools to do so. It stands, to this day, to be the hardest thing I've ever done. Getting underneath all my protective covering isn't easy. The sensitivity I possess scares me, mainly because I've ignored it most of my life. I've been hiding for too long.

After the meeting, I drive home. Sitting in my garden, I listen to the cheerful sounds of birds, punctuating delight in what could be considered a dark moment. I'm back to *how messed up am I?* How do I break free from the past?

"I want to live differently" are the words that fall from my mouth.

The phone rings. It's the middle school. "Hello, this is Meighan speaking," I answer.

"Ms. Leibert? We need you to come to the school to pick up your children."

"Are my kids okay?" I ask. My blood runs cold. Worry sets in.

"Yes, we will explain everything when you get here." The voice is clear and unemotional.

I drive as if I am in a daze, trying desperately to clear my head of negative thoughts. "You don't know anything yet. Stop thinking you do," I say defiantly to myself.

I arrive and go directly to the counselor's office, only because I know she has a relationship with Sebastian. She sees me in the doorway and stands up.

"Meighan, I love your son. I have such a soft spot in my heart for him," she says, concerned.

My insides crumble. *What is happening?* I cannot speak. My eyeballs scan the familiar office before I close them to allow my breaths to leave my body. I move to sit in the chair across from her desk, and she returns to her seat where my eyes lock with hers.

"He came in this morning and asked if he could talk with me. He lifted his shirt. I saw the bruises. He was kicked by his dad," she says in disgust. "Sebastian says it's been happening for a while. He doesn't want to go back. I called CPS right away, and they told me it wasn't enough. And I'm telling you I don't care. I phoned the police and made my own report." I can hear a note of triumph in her voice.

Sebastian, my eleven-year-old son, possesses the fortitude to stand up for himself, to change his reality. He knows how to ask for help.

A police officer comes to the door. Her red hair is pulled back into a ponytail, and she rests her hands on both sides of her belt. "Ms. Leibert?" she begins. "I'm Officer Ludlow. We want to issue an emergency protective order today. And to do that, we need you to take your children home," she says in a soft yet firm tone. "I will call you when it is done. Okay?"

I nod, realizing I can't exhale.

"Weighted Argument" by Grandma Margaret

"It is a blessing,"
 the wise mouths say.
"Much for the best."
 And yet, and yet—
 Life sings a song on the other side.
 Persuasive as sunrise,
 Or hunger,
 satisfied.

CHAPTER 15

SAGE

I receive sole custody in January 2018.

It delivers a different responsibility to my role as parent. Overwhelmed and relieved at the same time, I find myself determined to move us into a healthier state of existence. As their father slowly disappears, we are given the chance to wade through the imprint of hurt. I am inspired by the opportunity to change the course of our lives, to chart a different path.

And I am terrified. I felt alone during my marriage and stranded without it. Now I seem to be experiencing something else altogether, beyond words. It's like I am gripped by the echo of my past, the tradition of being left behind by the fathers who loved us into being. I want to break out and set us free.

With their dad exiting the picture, my kids are reliving a part of my own childhood. *How do they process all that's happened? Will I be enough for them?*

I am the only person holding myself back. When I use the words "I can't," what am I really saying? I need to change my relationship with fear. Instead of letting it incapacitate me, maybe I can use it to inspire.

I look at my past and dare to appreciate my evolution. Growing up has its own timeline. My maturation is slow. It takes me over fifty years to be okay with myself. Ownership comes late. and here I am.

A year later, I make a call on a whim to create a new experience for my triad. In the office of our family restaurant, I prepare for a conversation I've never had before. Looking out the window, my eyes travel across the water. The bay is flat with a large tanker, red and black, moving steadily along—slow, heavy, destination unknown.

Where am I headed?

My heart is beating fast with anticipation. I am both afraid and excited to have a conversation with Kelly Wendorf, owner of EQUUS in Santa Fe, New Mexico. I've been reading her blog for a few years and always imagined seeking her. *Today's the day.*

I bring the dream closer. I am intrigued and intimidated by the words I read on her website: "Innovative self-mastery and leadership development for individuals and organizations." My idea is to explore the possibility of taking my children with me.

"Hi, Kelly," I start, sitting upright in my seat and watching the tanker move out of sight. "My name is Meighan. I have two budding teenagers. My son Sebastian is twelve, and my daughter Francesca, also known as Frankie, is eleven. For years I've dreamed of coming to EQUUS, by myself, for myself. I want to know if you could design a program for me and my kids?" I say nervously, trying to stay calm.

Her voice is light and sweet. "Of course; we can do that. Tell me a little bit more about what you are seeking."

"Well," I say, unclear to what's important and insecure about complaining. "We've been through a lot," I tell her openly. "My marriage and divorce were intense." I hesitate and lower my voice as if I'm telling her a secret. "I am mostly surprised at how much I've hurt myself along the way."

Now I stop, not sure I can continue. Kelly doesn't say anything; she just lets the silence be. The space inspires me. "All three of us are on the mend—well, pausing really, maybe recalibrating. As my kids move into their teen years, I want to bolster connection and make our foundation solid. Is this something we might explore?"

I am now embarrassed by blathering on and notice I stopped breathing somewhere in the middle. I swallow a bunch of air too quickly, just in time to hear her response.

"Yes, absolutely. This all sounds wonderful and very brave of you to initiate." *Brave?* Here I am, thinking I'm not making any sense, and she just follows along.

"I'm excited," I say. "I'm also scared." The last word comes out a little softer. I choke back tears and feel the shift. I've opened the door to something new.

"Yes, change can feel scary," she affirms. "Just this conversation alone, Meighan, where you are asking for something different, for yourself and your children, will begin to upset your norm. Watch closely. Notice the changes that happen after we hang up. You've set something in motion." Her words give me comfort. I am surprised at how easy it is to have a conversation with someone who seems to understand me. Even though I am nervous, I do not feel ashamed for sharing my desire. *This just might be a first.*

We arrive in Santa Fe four days before Christmas. Frankie's unceasing moodiness is a drag. She cut her bangs a few days prior to our leaving and botched the job. She wears the crooked fringe unbelievably well and doesn't try to hide it in any way. I find this an amazing testament to her fortitude. Her ability to hold herself continues to astound me.

Currently I seem to be her metaphorical punching bag, and I take it personally. Because she is not one to talk about her feelings, I am stumped and know all I can do is give us both space, but none of it comes easy.

Frankie usually sleeps with me on vacations. On this trip, she wants to share her brother's bed, and a small part of me feels unwanted. Sebastian is frustrated with Frankie's behavior and finds it irritating. His protective nature impresses me, a mature inclination for a twelve-year-old.

I'm embarrassed by letting Frankie's attitude upset me. *Why can't I not care?* My dread increases as I discover our room has no hot water. A pipe had just burst before we arrived. All I wanted was a hot shower after our flight; now I will let that go.

I step out onto the veranda of our casitas to see all the furniture wrapped for winter. I look out to the land as far as my eyes travel. The sky looks like ice cream, a rainbow of sorbets, lemon into orange into raspberry, melting into the desert land.

I question what I have put into motion. *Am I asking too much of us?* Stripped from the comfort of home, I am challenged and forced to see myself in a different light. *Will I like what I find? How will I show up?*

The hotel I choose borders the EQUUS property, a mere two-minute drive. Kelly is waiting outside when we arrive. She stands about five-foot-seven, slight in frame, with short blond hair. Her wide smile welcomes us inside.

We follow Kelly into her home to be directed into a massive room with high ceilings and a giant wood-burning fireplace. The space is stunning in its simplicity and feels sacred. Four mats are positioned in a circle on the floor, and three hold a blanket, pillow, eye mask, and small journal. A crackling fire spreads heat throughout the room. A fourth mat is placed opposite the three, with the area between strewn with varying objects. I notice an abalone shell, a smudge stick of white sage, a large feather, a bowl, an assortment of small stuffed animals, a piece of stone or flint, and a lighter. A large drum sits off to the side.

"This is Shaman Niccole Toral," Kelly says. We see a dark-haired woman, not too tall, with a beautiful smile. "Hello," she says. "Please have a seat." Her gentle manner is calming. I detect a playfulness behind her bright eyes, stirring my curiosity.

Kelly moves to leave and says, "I will see you all tomorrow. Have a wonderful evening." As she steps out, a chill runs up my spine. My thoughts sour, tickled by worry. *What if my kids are obnoxious?*

I move toward the middle mat and sit down in a cross-legged position. Sebastian and Frankie choose their seats on either side of me.

Shaman Niccole sits across from us and tells us about smudging, a ceremonial practice for cleansing. She burns the sage leaves in the abalone shell, showing us how to wave the smoke toward and around our bodies. Her graceful movements quell my nervousness, and I get a sense of bathing in smoke so all the unnecessary bits travel elsewhere. She speaks of the power of intention and tells us that cleansing is the time to think about what we want to ask our spirit animal. Clearing our field through smudging will allow us to enter the ceremony grounded in clarity.

"This is where we begin," she says. "We prepare ourselves for the ceremony. We do this together." When she finishes smudging herself, she hands it to Sebastian. He copies what he saw Shaman Niccole do and then hands it to me. I love the way it smells. A sweet herbal smokiness surrounds me, strangely refreshing. Frankie is wide-eyed with anticipation as I hand her the shell.

Shaman Niccole brings our attention to the animals lying in the center of our circle and tells us spirit animals can take any form and we want to open to whatever shows up. "Carry your question with you, and be willing to ask for whatever guidance you want," she says. "Your spirit animal medicine is born with you. You can lean into your animals any time. They are here to support you during your lifetime." I am comforted by her words and realize I feel like I am at the beginning of a story. I sense the "once upon a time" flavor.

How do I become a better mom?

"Sequence" by Grandma Margaret

Light lies on the bay like ice.
The watery mirror,
reflecting a marble sky,
offers its stillness
to the birds.
Before the last brown leaf
Is blown from the branch,
The new buds of copper beech
Lift their slender spirals
in greeting.
One plum blossom
bursts from the tight pink cluster.
A gull runs down the wind
in sunshine.
What shall we plan?
I smell spring.

CHAPTER 16

TOTEM

We lie down, covering our bodies with blankets and adorning the eye masks. The darkness is cool and solid.

I feel Shaman Niccole standing nearby. Her voice travels through the air as she tells us, "There is no right or wrong way to do this. You need only pay attention to what shows up and stay curious. When you encounter an animal, ask them, 'Are you my spirit animal?' and listen for a yes."

I try to relax, but I seem preoccupied with my kids, whom I can't see. *Why am I so afraid to be with myself?* I settle into the floor and lean into the parts of my body that make contact, like my outer heels, my calves and thighs, the backside of my pelvis, my palms and elbows, my upper back and shoulders. I let everything get heavy and sink down. I soften my eyes under the mask and breathe slowly through my nose.

"When you feel ready, ask them your other question," she says. *How do I become a better mom?*

Shaman Niccole continues, "The answer may show up in language or images. Just be open to receive all of what arises. The tempo of the drumming will guide you in and through and eventually out. When the drumming slows, that is your signal to thank your spirit animal. Follow the path that brought you together, and come out the way you entered."

As I sit with her words, my mind is a jumble. I have nonsensical thoughts whirring through my head, distracting me. I am initially preoccupied with what my kids might be experiencing. Then I worry if I am doing it right, which I know is not supposed to be a concern. *What am I so insecure about? Can I fake it?* My insides are blustery. I continue to follow the lead of my panic. *What if it doesn't work?*

Following the drumbeats along the surface of my consciousness, something shifts…

I am walking through a forest toward a white sandy beach. I can see it in the distance, through the trees. I am repeating to myself that I am looking to meet my spirit animal. I play with the sand between my toes and am aware of feeling deeply happy. The bright sun sends warm kisses to my skin, and I feel beautiful and light and filled with joy. I'm laughing as I move myself into the water where I see a large orca. Her sleek black is shiny, and her glowing white sparkles. She beckons me forth. "Are you my spirit animal?" I say without moving my lips. "Yes," I hear in response. Her eyes tell me to come closer. She swallows me whole and pushes me out her spout, so I sit on her back as we travel through the blue of the ocean. I feel exhilarated by her speed and calmed by her presence. Her size is impressive. Repeating my intention of how to become a better mom grows into a desire for confidence. She tells me, "You naturally are. Just trust." She shows me I don't need more as we swim and jump and fly together. If anything, I get a message to lighten up, to be less serious. My wholeness is already here. "Accept it," she says. We jump high into the sky and dive deep into the water. I am lost in a wave of thrill. The freedom is magnificent, abundant, and strong.

The drum tempo changes, and a slower beat pulls me to the surface. I say goodbye to my spirit animal and thank her with my body as I hug her close. Happiness and gratitude spill from my pores. I walk myself back through the sand and the forest and find my body. Immediately surprised and relieved by my experience, I follow the beats. *Did I fall asleep? Was that a dream?*

When we sit up, Niccole asks us to journal for a few minutes to capture our visions. When we finish writing, we are invited to share our experiences. Sebastian wants to go first. My whole body expands when I listen to my children. I am riveted by their telling.

Sebastian recounts his experience in his animated way, excited for the attention. "I'm running through the woods and see all these different creatures, like birds, frogs, snakes, and raccoons. I keep asking them, 'Are you my spirit animal?' Nobody says anything really. Then I see some boys fighting, and I step closer to them. 'What's going on?' I ask, thinking I might be able to help, and they both look at me. Then a big bear shows up behind one of the boys and roars. The boys run away. I look up at him and ask, 'Are you my spirit animal?' The bear answers yes and asks me to climb up on his shoulders. When I'm up there I feel so good and happy. Then I ask him my other question: 'How do I believe in myself?' And he roars out loud and starts to run fast. 'You are who you are just as you are, exactly as you are meant to be. I am always here to help you know this. Being true is the only way. Pay attention to when you falter and give up on yourself so you can find your way back.'"

Looking at him, I see his beauty in a different way. His sensitivity has always been strong. His desire to help the fighting boys shows he is not afraid to put himself out there and get involved. His question surrounding confidence is a yearning as old as time.

Shaman Niccole tells Sebastian that grizzly bear is his totem.

"Grizzly is a symbol of freedom," she says, "of strength and understanding. He is a healer and a teacher."

I think about Sebastian and how much of his personality fits with this description. I like seeing him in this light.

"Grizzly teaches us the importance of taking a stand," Shaman Niccole continues, "and commanding power in a healthy way. Grizzly represents a keen sense of knowing, strength, confidence, standing against adversity, taking action and leadership, healing self and others, the importance of solitude, and provides strong grounding forces. Grizzly bear leads by caring."

Sebastian soaks up the attention, and I can tell it makes him feel good.

"Sebastian," Shaman Niccole says while picking up a small piece of something in front of her. "I went hiking yesterday, and I found this arrowhead. It is a symbol of direction. In finding it, I understand I am meant to give it to you, so you may have something to guide you forward." She hands it to Sebastian.

"What's an arrowhead?" he asks gently.

"It is usually a carved piece of stone attached to an arrow. It's used for hunting," she answers, watching Sebastian.

He moves the piece around his fingers and looks at it closely. "It's very old," she adds.

Seeing my son treasured by this woman we just met fills me with appreciation. I catch a glimpse of the magic of seren-dipity—how Shaman Niccole's finding the arrowhead and perhaps her tuning into the meaning of it could bring her to this moment with Sebastian. It is possible everything we experience can be a message, if we choose to see it that way.

Shaman Niccole turns her gaze to Frankie and asks if she would like to share her experience. Frankie has so much energy she practically needs to stand up so she can tell her story with her whole body. She drops her head before she begins, a sign of shyness, an all-too-familiar moment used to gather her courage.

"I'm walking in a forest, and I see a bunch of different paths to take. I decide to go down the middle road. I see a frog, then a deer, then a bird. I ask all of them if they are my spirit animal. They all shake their heads. I keep walking, and a bunch of animals surround me. They are short, long, and skinny. We jump around and play. It is so much fun. We are laughing and dance around until they pick me up and carry me. They bring me to a cave, and I see a larger version of what they look like. She is elegant and shiny, bright with gold color. So I ask her, 'Are you my spirit animal?' and she says yes. She pulls me into her lap, and we tickle each other. I ask her my other question, 'How do I be okay with what I want when other people don't like it?' She spins me around on my stomach and strokes my back as she tells me, 'Only you can decide for yourself. Pleasing others only works if it pleases you too. Every time you go against what feels right for you, you ignore your knowing, which is most valued. Trust yourself, and all will be well.'"

I am moved by Frankie's story and thrilled to hear her experience. Here she is, my little girl, connecting with the playful part of her I know all too well and discovering her own knowing is strong.

"Frankie," Shaman Niccole says. "Ferret is your totem."

Frankie immediately asks, "What's a ferret?"

Shaman Niccole reaches for a white stuffed animal in front of her and gives it to Frankie. It is long and skinny with a pointed nose. Frankie is beaming as she holds the furry creature close to her body.

Shaman Niccole continues to share that ferrets teach us how to endure and thrive. They love to play, explore, and interact with other creatures. Ferrets express qualities of slyness, secretiveness, cleverness, energetic, wisdom, focus, illusion, playfulness, discernment, and wit.

"The central message of ferret," Shaman Niccole says, "is to remember how to play. You need a break for laughter and wonder."

I think about this and admire how well it fits with Frankie's temperament and personality.

We continue to learn that the ferret totem needs a personal hidey hole. When life becomes chaotic, retreat and rest become vital. Ferrets exhibit great intelligence and analytical ability, and they reflect earth elements of staying grounded, decisive thinking, diplomacy, and mediation. Ferrets live in the moment and soak up all the yumminess.

Knowing my kids' medicine deepens my understanding of them in a way. These beings are not mine, per se; they belong to the universe. *Can I really admit that to myself? Can I finally separate us in a healthy way?* I am ashamed by my former need to hide behind them and my role as their mom. It was all so desperate.

They are the missing ingredients to provide a different love experience from the one I've known.

After I share my journey, Niccole tells me orcas are highly intelligent with great learning abilities, adaptable, and up for the challenge. Orcas derive strength through community and wise comradery. They operate in matriarchal pods, survive in the harshest of conditions, and inspire great awe from others. Orcas are fierce protectors of their family and clan. Orcas have a direct connection to larger and more rarified energies of the universe and the cosmos. Because of this, orca people do well to allow those energies to come and support, rather than to do it alone and achieve goals through sheer effort and intention.

As I listen to what she describes I have a strong desire to stop my automatic thinking that has me believing I am wrong or need to do everything alone. I am intrigued by this "direct connection" to the universe and wonder how I might understand more. As I relax myself into this experience, I lean into the strength of my orca totem to find a new motivation toward love, nourishing, and healing.

These descriptions uncover our core personas and accentuate our natural wisdom. All three of us are challenged by social conditioning, and we get bogged down with a boatload of shoulds. *Who are we, and what really matters?* Taking the time to know ourselves without that burden to remember a different way feels possible.

"First Snow" by Grandma Margaret

Wakeful at Midnight
I listen to silence.
The snowfall muffles my ears,
lies heavy on the roof,
blinds the windows of my room.
When, at last,
I move through the stillness,
to open a dark door,
I stand
Sightless, where all is white!
Deaf,
in the embracing hush;
Wordless in wonder
at such hoary majesty.

CHAPTER 17

HERD WISDOM

The next few days are spent with the EQUUS herd of horses and one donkey. Before we engage, we set intentions. Kelly has us gather in a small room and open our journals. She asks us to get quiet, dig deep, and pull forth something we want for ourselves.

"Write it down so you can refer to it often. Start with the words 'I want to know,'" she says. She leaves the room to give us privacy.

I watch my children write with fervor. We share our intentions out loud before Kelly returns. We are gentle with our truths, and I am impressed with my children's willingness.

Meighan: I want to know I am enough.

Sebastian: I want to know I am special.

Frankie: I want to know my way is okay—to not be perfect for everyone else or to feed into their expectations.

I swallow hard and choke back tears. I can relate to their desires. I think how we are all the same, regardless of age. Sharing these truths is a powerful connector. In this moment, we are seeing each other and the beginning of a valuable learning. No matter how much I know my son is special and my daughter's way is okay, they need to believe it for themselves. Their questions are a beautiful sign.

Kelly walks us out of the building and toward the arena. We see the horses; some are standing, and a few are lying down. Outside the gate, my kids' excited wonder bounces off their bodies. None of us have experience with horses. I am a bit uneasy.

Kelly points with her fingers to each horse and tells us their name. "We'll step inside and see who has an interest in you three. Okay?"

We are chosen by our teachers. The four of us move through the gate. I step away from Sebastian and Frankie, unsure of what I'm doing. They both slowly walk without hesitation toward the herd, which I figure is a good sign.

"That's Dante," says Kelly of the white horse nearing Sebastian. His nose has a particular curve I do not see on the other horses.

Frankie is beaming with a smile so brightly her face is red. It's hard for me to remember the cold shoulder she gave me last night amid this new vibrant delight. A beautiful chestnut brown horse is a few feet away, and I watch Frankie extend her hands in greeting.

"That's Cisco, Frankie," says Kelly. "Go ahead. It's okay."

Cisco moves closer to let Frankie touch her.

With my eyes closed I feel a presence behind me. As my eyes open, I make a slight turn to see a large, beautiful creature standing before me.

"Meighan," Kelly says. "Looks like Artemis has chosen you. She is the leader of the herd, another mom of sorts. You are in good company."

Kelly moves everyone out of the arena, so Artemis and I are alone. My heart is thumping, I am filled with terror and discomfort. I am also wrapped up in a hopeful dream for a miracle. If I am the broken piece, Artemis will be the super glue.

In a split second I am transported back in time, remembering my ten-year-old self in a barn, and a horse nips my thigh. The move is sudden, quick, and paralyzes me as I stand still, afraid to move. Swallowing the shock and the pain, I hold back my tears, determined to put forth a brave front. The bruise, a mark of shame, takes weeks to heal. This is the memory I carry with me into the arena with Artemis. *Please don't bite me.*

Artemis does not seem interested. She keeps her distance as I wade through my internal turmoil. Kelly tells me, "She knows you're here. See how her ears move back and forth?" I stand still and scan my insides: confusion, fear, hope. *What am I doing here?* I ask myself. *What do I want?* I continue to squirrel through my thoughts and feelings. Artemis picks up her head and looks at me. I slip into silently begging for her attention, a mediocre prayer to help me save face. *Who am I trying to please?*

I switch gears. *I am here because I feel broken. I am scared and unsure.* Artemis moves toward me. My admission brings tears, and Artemis comes closer. As I let my walls crumble, I open the space between us. We begin to walk. I keep hearing the words "no doubt."

Our interaction feels slippery. We are together, and then we're not. This helps me witness my half-heartedness—a subtle moment of seeming to lose connection with myself and thinking she will carry us. When Artemis disengages, I am left to feel into my part. It's as if my action severs the cord that united us. *Is that it?*

I know how to hope for something to happen without taking any responsibility. My fear is attached to a belief that what I want is not allowed. Artemis shows me with her yawning, a sign of support, that being myself fully, undistracted, is the only way. The simplicity of it seems unreal—maybe even impossible. And here I am relating with a giant animal to learn, for the first time in my life, that I am okay.

Only when I own my intention and direction do we find harmony. Artemis teaches me to get clear. A few times I have to check in, get quiet, and touch base. She shows me I know what I need. *Oh my god.* In this space we connect deeply, and I can listen. *Oh,* I think, *where I am coming from holds the power.*

When I give myself permission to be myself, I am positively oriented. Artemis shows me the gift of attunement. Without it, my communication doesn't translate. I end up sending mixed messages.

Through this nonverbal equine experience, I am exposed to some deep inner knowledge. Artemis's gentle persistence and ability to hold space act like an anchor. It is my greatest learning. I exhibit strength in being.

Kelly tells me before I leave, "Meighan, the best kind of creation we manifest, whether in our personal lives or in larger settings, is creation informed by wholeness—a fusion between our oneness with spirit, our yearning for the good of all, and our own heart's desire. When we harness our thoughts and intentions to that nexus, we become powerful and honorable agents of change."

We all hug several times upon our departure. I wave goodbye and say openly, "We'll be back." I mean it. Being here feels important, and I want to continue my education.

As Kelly promised, our lives dramatically shift in the following months. My investment to live the life of my dreams inspires me with clear conscience to pave a new way forward for my tribe.

"Identity" by Grandma Margaret

Am I my clothes?
My house, the things I own?
The books I read,
or the flower in my garden?
Can you unearth me
in the scraps of wood and rusty iron,
that beach, and barn, and street
throw up as trash,
and I select as treasure?
Will I remain, if all these parts of me,
Alter or vanish,
as such objects do?
And lacking this assemblage of debris,
Need nothing else,
to be in truth,
Myself?

CHAPTER 18

BECOMING

Reflecting on what has come before isn't easy, but I want to tell my mom what happened on my eighteenth birthday. We're seated together in the small oasis she calls her garden. Jasmine vines weave in and around the trellised walls, their fragrance floating through the air. We've made mussels with garlic butter and have champagne, just because.

I'm not sure how to ease into this conversation, so I don't bother.

"Mom," I start, hesitantly, struggling to find the words. "My first time having sex was not consensual," I say, jumping right in with both feet. "It happened on my eighteenth birthday. I was raped. For so long I just considered it my first time. It's been a big emotional mess to unravel, and I just wanted you to know because, well, you're my mom."

She drops her chin and looks at the table between us. "Me too."

"What?" I say, surprised and newly upset.

"I was a freshman in college. My professor invited me into his office after class. I was a virgin. I didn't know what to do," she tells me in a soft voice. She seemed reduced to her young self, over sixty years ago. I sense the shame and confusion surrounding something she couldn't control. *Crap*, I think. *No fucking way I am hearing this.*

"My dad found out," she continues. "He wanted to help me, but I don't think he really knew how. He told me my professor was a married man, with a family. I had no idea." Mom's voice sounds young, and it surprises me to see her this way.

"Wait," I interrupt her. "Mom, what are you saying? Your dad took his side?"

"No, I don't think so," she says softly. "Dad didn't criticize me, but he needed me to understand my professor's family was the priority. It was confusing." I place my hand on hers and hold it while my insides collapse. I never knew my grandpa. He died before my parents married.

"Mom, I'm so sorry that happened to you," I say in a quiet voice.

She looks at me and raises her glass. "Cheers to surviving and moving on," she says strongly.

Uncomfortably, I pick up my glass and clink hers. "Yes, Mom. Cheers." I want to ask her why she never told me before, why she didn't think to use her story to influence my own understanding of sex. Maybe she didn't know how, or it was just too painful. Regardless, a gigantic truth sits heavily in my lap.

"My moving on hasn't been so seamless, Mom," I begin. I'm not sure I have the guts to keep going. "Sex was not a pleasurable experience for most of my life. The rape made me think it was supposed to be like that." I sense my words are lost on her. I am uncomfortable with what I've shared and choose to leave it alone. Maybe now is the time to enjoy each other's company in the shade of the afternoon.

On my drive home, I dig deep and reflect. Most of my life is colored by my attempt to be like everybody else while ignoring internal messages. I am not familiar with understanding my own needs or advocating on my own behalf. My duty or loyalty or commitment to others kept me tied to pleasing the people around me.

Sitting with the truth of our past is heavy. Running away is something I've done most of my life because for so long I wished I had a different story. Still, I clung to it, quietly and fiercely, as a means for explanation and definition. Without knowing, I let it confine me.

My trip to EQUUS planted seeds for new understanding and introduced me to a new question: What am I running to, and how will I assert myself in my new story?

Opening the doors that present themselves is the first step. I begin to say yes and follow the crumbs.

Kelly Wendorf sends me an invitation to join a wisdom circle of eight members. My insecurity does not hold me back, and I commit to the six-month exploration. We meet regularly and share our discoveries. I'm asked to set an intention, and I choose two: to be free to make my own choices without feeling guilty and to discover a new career path. I want to make enough money doing something that is a clear authentic expression of my values.

We hold hands, virtually, through the onset of COVID-19. We feel the depth of our connection from the beginning. In this group I share my dream of writing a book. I wake up one morning with a clear message. The title of the book is inspired by my dad: *The Man I Didn't Know*. Change starts with listening to my ideas with kindness instead of criticism. The gratitude our group grows is an anchoring addition to all the "upside down" we experience generated by the pandemic.

Several life coaches are in the group. I have no reference for this type of work, and my curiosity explodes.

I initially ask one of them to coach my family and explain I am seeking support to bond us during preteen chaos. I can barely remember this stage in my own life, and the current personality twists in our household create dissonance. Confusion and irritation can suck us down the rabbit hole. As a single parent, I am forever seeking positive structures for us to lean on.

I learn if I receive coaching alone, my transformation will benefit my kids. I spend six months working with a professional coach to discover my values, which helps me acknowledge myself in new ways. I am mesmerized by the positive and honest nature of this one-on-one dynamic.

My coach was trained with the Co-Active Training Institute (CTI). I find the course online and plan to do the same. I book CTI Fundamentals in April 2020 and discover a tribe of like-minded beings. Five courses through the program encourage my shift. I spend a year studying online in the middle of the night, when my house is quiet, taking classes on a European time zone to get certified as a life coach.

Actively exploring my interests impacts my family. As I find more people who share my philosophies around healing, my confidence grows. Widening my social network is medicinal. Standing upright in my own shoes enhances my recovery, which naturally and beautifully influences my parenting.

Now I am ready to remember what I chose to forget. Two memories come forward.

"To A Line Drawing" by Grandma Margaret

Spare, and liquid,
and absolutely irreversible.
One can add a bit, perhaps,
but never take away.
You comment, rather than describe;
Fragmenting life, in search of essence.
Space enclosed,
or extended to linear infinity,
I find a whole philosophy
within your smallest squiggle.

CHAPTER 19

PEPPERMINTS AND COBWEBS (MEMORIES)

SIX YEARS OLD

Wrapping my tiny fingers around the headboard, I grip tightly to kick my legs into the air. When I let go, I reach my arms overhead to see how high I can jump. I'm with my brother and another friend, both two years younger than me. Mom's bed squeaks with our ruckus. We lose our balance and fall into each other as we go down.

I feel so free, pushing my feet into her mattress to spring myself up toward the ceiling. I'm small, so it feels like I'm flying. I don't want to stop.

Our faces are red. We keep falling onto our backs and laughing out loud before we start again.

My babysitter's boyfriend walks into the room and stands by the side of the bed. He smells funny. He's hairy. His hair is brownish in color, falling from his head, smeared across his face, and sprouting out the top of his shirt. It's everywhere.

"Come here, all of you. Line yourselves up on the edge." We hear him, but we don't really want to stop playing. We continue to squirm and giggle.

"Just stand still," he says. "Get over here."

I am the oldest and the tallest, so I go first.

Putting his hands on my waist to keep me from moving, he says, "Now close your eyes and open your mouth."

"Why?"

"I'll show you," he says smiling.

I close my eyes, and I don't really want to open my mouth. His hands squeeze a little tighter.

"Just stick out your tongue."

"Why?" I ask softly, opening my eyes.

"Okay, let's play a game. If you touch your tongue to my tongue, I will give you a piece of candy."

"I don't want to do that."

He digs into his pocket and pulls out peppermints, the red-and-white striped kind. They are not my favorite. They're too minty and sting my tongue. I prefer milk chocolate.

My brother and friend start jumping up and down, screaming, "Candy! Yay! Candy!"

He stands there and sticks out his tongue. I lean forward and touch it with mine. It's warm. I jump back and squeal, "Ew!" It tastes strange, kind of sour. A smell makes me pinch my nose.

"Do you like it?" he asks.

"No," I say, wishing I wasn't here anymore.

"Do you want to do it again?" he asks me with a face that doesn't look happy.

"No," I repeat.

"C'mon, let's do it again. I'll make it better this time. Promise." He lifts his chest a bit when he says this. His eyes drill holes in my cheeks.

He pulls me close and covers my mouth with his. The heat of his breath turns my stomach, and I can't get free. His tongue moves my lips apart. I'm stuck here. When he lets me go, he throws the candy from his pocket on the bed.

I'm scared.

I grab my blankie and sit behind the pillows on my mom's bed. I'll stay until she comes home. Slipping the first two fingers of my left hand into my mouth, I abandon myself to sucking, waiting for my dreams to take hold.

Doubt creeps under my skin. There's nowhere for me to put it, so I secret it away.

EIGHT YEARS OLD

I share a bedroom with my brother. We each have a single bed on opposite sides of the room, parallel to each other.

Mom lets us draw on our walls, and they are covered with our imaginings. The room is big with lots of space to play. I like being barefoot because the shag carpet is fun to grab with my toes.

My laundry hamper, a rattan basket, sits under a table at the far end of the room. I organized my dirty clothes earlier and discovered I had no clean pajamas.

I wait for my brother to get into bed before I slip naked under my covers. I like the softness of the sheets over my skin. I giggle with excitement. I flip onto my stomach and put my hands under my pillow to find my blankie. I turn my head in the direction of my brother; but I can barely see anything through the dark of the room.

Turning onto my back, I close my eyes and count sheep. I imagine them jumping over a fence. Some have curly hair and others have straight. One is full of braids and another has ponytails with pink ribbons. I hear music and laughter coming from the living room. Mom has friends over.

Sucking my fingers and holding my blankie close, I settle myself into a rhythm of breathing that lulls me to sleep. Held deep in slumber, I dance with angels.

Startled awake, my eyes burst open in the dark. I am aware of fingers gliding across the surface of my naked body. These alien digits are soft and delicate. I don't understand. His touch is gentle, like he is teasing knots out of cobwebs. I am terrified. I hold my breath.

The sound that comes out of my mouth is a short scream muffled by a gasp. My heart moves into my throat. I grab my covers, pull them close, and sit up.

My sounds go unanswered, swallowed by the dark. With eyes stretched wide, I can't see anything. Unsure of what to do, I stay there, bunched up and afraid. I hear him moving in the room. He pauses in the doorway, my eyes staring straight ahead to see his body pierce the pale light streaming from the corridor. Strands of my innocence follow him into the hall.

I need clothes. Wrapping myself in my sheet, I move to the hamper to find dirty pajamas. Once I'm dressed, I begin to wail.

"Mom! Mom! *Mom!*" I scream, trying to make it louder than the music. I stop when I am too tired to continue.

I can't sleep.

Removing blankets and pillows from my bed, I move into the room next to ours. Two closets line the far wall. I open the one on the left, farthest from our bedroom. It has an accordion door, making the right side sandwich into the left side. Under the hanging clothes I find space just big enough for me to lie down. Surrounded by the three walls, I fill the small space and feel snug. No longer exposed, I surrender myself to sleep. I stay here for months, until I am ready to return to my big-girl bed.

"Reciprocity" by Grandma Margaret

I want you to destroy my solitude
Invade it with your body,
Demolish it with your words,
And give up, in turn,
Your solitude;
For banishment in me.

CHAPTER 20

KAYAK

After remembering moments from my childhood, I believe it's possible parts of me shut down as a means of protection. I have this idea that some guidance might be useful and work with a therapist trained in somatic experiencing to help connect me with my body. I am unpracticed at tracking my senses but take direction well. During my first session I get lost in all the details of my interior, traveling between the layers of my skin and following what I think might be blood flow. In one short hour I am introduced to a new world of me and get completely hooked.

I've spent most of my life ignoring what is here, whether it be an upset stomach or an urgent sense to do something. Taking time to sit with myself, to recognize what's happening within teaches me my body is my biggest ally. By nature, it responds to everything around me. I need only to feel and listen. Being introduced to my internal intelligence sparks a new and valuable relationship, one I've been missing.

My therapist tells me how smart my little girl self was to move into the closet, to create a space of safety. It was just big enough to hold me, like an incubator. Her language encourages me to look with new eyes to events in my past and to cultivate appreciation for my strength and perseverance. I broaden my sensory awareness and listen, smell, taste, visualize, and connect with whatever shows up.

These extra details become anchors in my experience as I ride surfacing emotional waves. My nervous system shifts into a relaxed state. For the first time in my life, I like being with myself and discover comfort in stillness that welcomes me home.

As I become more adept at being with my emotions, I am not as inclined to separate them out, making me less fractured and compartmentalized. This act of integration delivers wholeness and I find a life force too long ignored.

Through this work my adult self acknowledges my inner child in all her confusion, and we heal, together. She runs into my arms, and I tell her, "I am here, and I love you. I am sorry this happened, and you will be okay. Look who you grow up to be—a mom with two amazing kids."

This new state of feeling influences my curiosity about my dad. I revisit the book idea I woke up with last year and decide to pursue it with new fervor. My first thought is to pick my mom's brain.

I make a date with her to go kayaking in China Camp, one of our favorite spots for family gatherings. She checks the tides, and we plan for 10:00 a.m. Her truck brings the kayaks. I'm in charge of snacks. I have cans of Modelo, bottled water, egg salad, and tortilla chips. While we are unloading the boats, I tell her what I'm after.

"Mom, I want to know more about your and Dad's story. Do you think you can fill in some of the gaps for me?" I ask.

"I can try," she answers. "It was a long time ago." Her hair is a silvery, bright white now, and it looks so pretty on her. I wonder if my hair will do the same. She swims every day and keeps herself fit, strong, and agile. I'm a little surprised and glad she lets me help with the boats.

My mom was born Alexa Maria Peralta, the longest most beautiful name I've ever heard, and everyone knows her as Flicka. The nickname was given to her as a child and it stuck, just another remarkable signature of her immeasurable uniqueness. I smile and think, *My Friend Flicka*. It's true; she is an exceptional human being and a great pal.

She and Frankie spent yesterday afternoon walking through North Beach to get lunch. "Mom," Frankie says to me, "what should have taken maybe twenty minutes to get to the restaurant took over an hour. Grandma knows everybody, and our whole walk was interrupted with, 'Hi, Flicka,' so we stopped to speak to so many people. It was crazy!"

I look over at Mom now, smiling. She spent a lifetime invested in community. She's a powerful role model. I'm looking forward to hearing how she and Dad got started.

"Yeah, I know. Whatever you can give me will be great," I say with relief. I was open to her not wanting to talk about it at all.

Looks like we picked a perfect day. The water is flat, shimmering in the sunlight and smooth as glass. Mom pushes her kayak into the water and jumps in. "Let's head out to the left so we can have the tide push us back," she says, paddling.

"Okay," I answer, moving as fast as I can to catch up with her. Already in her late sixties, she moves faster than I do.

When I think I am in earshot, I say, "Just start from the beginning. I need a little back story." Next to each other, we soon find our rhythm.

"I met your dad at UC Berkeley. He was getting his master's degree in dramatic arts. I was an undergrad studying painting," she tells me. I strain to hear what she's saying and almost topple over.

"I thought you studied architecture," I interrupt.

"That was freshman year. Then I studied in Rome as a sophomore. I met your dad when I was a junior, and painting was my focus."

"Were you living at home or at school?" I ask.

"I wasn't at home," she says with a sigh.

"When did your dad die, Mom?" I ask carefully.

"He died my junior year," she says, dropping her chin toward her chest in a silent prayer. "That was a hard time."

I let this information sit between us for a bit. A wave of embarrassment washes over me. I've never seen my mom as vulnerable and in pain. She's always struck me as strong and confident, even in tough times. Seeing her softer side in this light deepens my understanding of her and my love.

Taking the time to imagine my mom's childhood makes me sad. Her mom was controlling and made her do stuff she didn't like. Her older sister ran away at seventeen, leaving Mom alone in a house of confusion when she was only fourteen.

Mom told me once, "I had two mommies growing up. One was nice, and the other was mean. I never knew which one was going to be there in the morning or meet me after school." I can't imagine how hard that must've been for her. Grandma was diagnosed with bipolar disorder in her late seventies, which explained all the chaos mom suffered as a kid. Grandma was violent, which is why my aunt left.

"Meeting Michael was exciting," she says, accidentally splashing me with water. The cool drops are welcome as I'm starting to get hot. I think about jumping in for a swim but don't know if I'll be able to get back in the boat.

We paddle past the pier and head north at a gentle speed. Mom waves her arm toward land. Sea lions cover the rocks where sun rays bounce off silky skins, making their bodies glisten like diamonds.

The repeating rhythm of my oar slicing forward into the water and moving backward holds my focus. Here we are, two women gliding along together, connected by blood and love and history. We both lost our dads when we were teenagers, yet we've never discussed the impact of that pain. *We share loss.* The truth of this feels immense. My mom has her own protective covering, just like me.

"Mom," I say quietly, "will you tell me about your dad?"

"He loved women," she says, looking out at the water ahead of us. "I just remember that. He enjoyed being with them. And he wasn't around much. He came home for dinner every night, but other than that, he was off doing whatever he was doing."

"Sounds kind of like my dad," I offer in solidarity.

"Yeah. Your dad loved women too," she says reflectively. "He was also never home. Well, not in a way that helped." Mom pauses here and looks at me. I offer a small smile.

"He was talented and interesting, a great storyteller. I loved his voice," she tells me with admiration. "Mind you, I was eighteen and he was twenty-three when we met, so to me, he seemed mature and sophisticated." Her face broadens and her eyes twinkle before she adds, "Your dad introduced me to the joys of drinking."

"Oh yeah? Where was that?" I ask. The sun feels so good. Being out here alone with my mom makes me appreciate how lucky we are to live in the Bay Area.

"The bars in North Beach, of course. Your dad was good friends with Deanna and Sean," she tells me for the first time. They were the owners of Mooney's Irish Pub on Grant Avenue, only a few blocks from where we lived. It was our second living room.

She laughs. "Michael asked me to marry him while sitting at the bar." I laugh too. Oh, to be a fly on the wall back then. "I was quite thrilled. That's why I said yes," she finishes.

"Wow, Mom, you were so young," I say softly.

"I was. And my mother was not happy about any of it. She had dreams of me marrying a New York lawyer. Showing up with Michael, a man in theater, almost gave her a heart attack. And I just couldn't care," she finishes.

I follow Mom's lead, and we move toward shore. I am ready for a break. My arms are exhausted. We drag the boats up the beach and sit with our feet in the water. The sky above shows streaks of clouds brushing across a pale blue sky. I hand Mom a beer—Modelo is our favorite—and open the container of egg salad to place it next to the chips between us.

After she takes a sip, Mom says, "Thanks. This is good."

"Where did you go on your honeymoon?" I ask.

"We spent a few weeks traveling through Morocco, Casa Blanca, and Agadir," she croons, as though it was as adventurous as the names sound. I've never been to any of these places and applaud her daring at such a young age. "Then we landed in Delphi, Greece, where we lived for one year," she says.

"That sounds amazing, Mom. Why so long?"

"It was all part of your dad's plan with the UC Berkeley Drama Department. He was to perform the lead role in the play *Hector* by Euripides, the first ever production in a Greek amphitheater," she tells me as she looks out at the water in front of us.

Mom seems lost in the past. I love listening to her remember. "Being with your dad was fun, Meighan," she says, turning her head toward me. "Let's head back."

"Being with you is fun, Mom," I say.

I put our empty cans and foodstuffs in the bag I brought. After securing it in the kayak, I jump in and start paddling away from shore. Then we let the current push us along. Mom closes her eyes and enjoys the heat of the sun. I do the same. I say gently, "What was it like, Mom?"

"It was great, totally out there," she tells me. "Once we got to Delphi, we found an apartment that had one cold water tap and a toilet outhouse to the left of the front door. I loved it!"

"Really? It wasn't too rustic for you?" I ask.

"Not at all. I don't care about stuff like that," she says. She looks so relaxed and at home on her kayak. I turn my face to the sun and sigh with joy. Maybe growing up with too much stuff can make you not need all the details. Even now, she lives in quite the unconventional space, open and unstructured.

It strikes me how much of what we learn comes from our parents, whether we like it or not.

"We threw amazing naked dinner parties and drank delicious red wine," she continues. "Your dad was a fabulous cook. Did you know that? He taught me." She laughs and winks. "That's what carried us through."

After my parents divorced in 1971, Mom and her best friend started cooking brunches on Sundays for Mooney's customers. Articles in the local newspaper touted their success. It was unheard of for debutantes to work. Young women of their stature were expected to marry and start families. Soon thereafter, the Cooking Company was born, a thriving catering business that eventually led them to becoming restaurateurs, and Pier 23 Cafe opened in 1985. When we opened Sweetie's Art Bar in 2000, Mom and I would cook the daily lunches. I'd walk down the hill from the Art Institute, where I was working toward my BA in painting, and we'd make fresh mussels or clams or whatever we felt like eating. This lasted for about a month until we realized opening time needed to be 4:00 p.m.

Relaxed and floating alongside each other, I am full of love and wonder. *My mom is a pioneer.* I hear her shift in her kayak and open my eyes. She sits up and looks over at me. We start paddling. We don't talk for a while and enjoy the quiet.

"Mom," I say, breaking the silence. "Why did you get divorced? Who initiated it?" I ask a bit reluctantly because I don't want to make her sad.

"I did. What we were doing didn't seem like a marriage. It wasn't what I imagined for myself. Your dad had a girlfriend, and I didn't like it," she admits.

"Do you think Grandpa had other women too?" I ask.

"I think it's possible," she says. "What else would he be doing?"

High tide floats us ashore, and we have less beach to travel to load our kayaks. I am deep in thought with the stories from our past as we secure the vessels in the back of the truck.

"Thanks, Mom. I have a better picture of your love story," I say, wrapping my arms around her. "I'm lucky to have amazing parents." I kiss her on the cheek and add, "I love you."

"I love you too," she says.

I wait until she drives out of the parking lot to sit on the picnic table in front of my car. Watching the water helps me organize my thinking, and I line up the truth of what I know. Infidelity is a marker in my family history. My own husband found his next wife while still married to me. Is it possible we repeat what we choose to ignore?

I don't like admitting I take my mom for granted and make a note to try to acknowledge her more in my day-to-day. Her unique influence is a wonderful marker in my life. When it comes to my childhood, I seem more focused on what I didn't get from my parents than anything else. I don't want to live like that anymore.

This reminds me of the first time I bought Mom a single rose after school.

(circa 1950's) Leibert Brothers from left David, John, Michael

1957 Dad's senior high school yearbook photo

1960 Dad

1965 Grandma Margaret with Michael and Flicka on their wedding day

1966 Dad, Trattoria Delphi

1967 Meighan with Mom and Dad

1968 Set Building, College Avenue, image courtesy of
the Berkeley Repertory Theatr

1968 The Theatre on College Avenue image courtesy of
the Berkeley Repertory Theatre

1968 The Theatre, image courtesy of the Berkeley Repertory Theatre

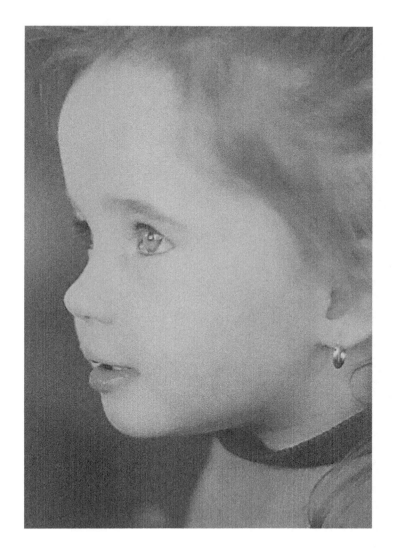

1969 Meighan

1970 Meighan

1975 Grandma Margaret and Dad

1975 Meighan

1977 Meighan

1978 "Buy-A-Brick Campaign" for the new theater on
Addison Street, theater courtyard

1978 Flicka and Meighan

1980 Dad, image courtesy of the Berkeley Repertory Theatre

1980 McGurrin Leibert and Tony Amendola in "My Heart's in the Highlands", image courtesy of the Berkeley Repertory Theatre

1980, The Company, McGurrin Leibert in 2nd row,
image courtesy of the Berkeley Repertory Theatre

1984 Meighan junior varsity basketball

1985 Meighan high school graduation

Meighan's 1985 high school senior yearbook page

2017, family reunited, we find Dad and discover his grandaughter was born on the date he died, October 29.

"Wakeful" by Grandma Margaret

Moonlight draws symbols on my curtains,
I am filled with the wonder,
and cannot sleep.
Gently the sea is speaking,
Beyond a dark headland.
I listen carefully,
but do not understand.
Will meaning always elude me?

CHAPTER 21

STERLING (MEMORY)

I scrounge the house for money, collecting pennies, nickels, dimes, and if I'm lucky, a quarter. I rummage through pockets of clothes, both dirty and clean. All I need is one dollar and twenty-five cents.

After school I like to visit the flower shop near the bus stop. Today, I prefer roses. Mom told me her favorite flower was a rose, and that's what I hope to find.

My eyes are immediately drawn to a bunch of pale lavender roses surrounded by an array of other colors—reds, yellows, pinks, and whites. They are stunning. "Maybe this is considered a young purple," I think out loud.

A tall man with dark hair steps toward me slowly. Dressed in a yellow button-down shirt, green corduroys, and loafers, he adds brightly, "Sterling is its name—a very special rose."

"My dad says red roses are for love and yellow roses are for friendship. What does a pale purple rose represent?" I ask eagerly. I want a rose that means everything, all at once.

"Sterling roses represent enchantment and grace," he tells me, moving closer to where I am standing. "Who's it for?"

"My mom. I want to show her how much she means to me." I pause before I continue. "Can you tell me what grace and enchantment mean?"

"Ah," says the nice man. "That is a fun question." He looks at the bucket of sterling roses and takes a deep breath in before he begins. "Enchantment is the magic of fairytales, my sweet girl, and grace is simple elegance."

"Elegance?" I ask.

"Style, my dear, is something we all want," he says with a twinkle in his eye.

"Thank you. I'm excited to know a flower could mean so many things!" I exclaim. I look at the gentle curve of the petals and say softly, "It's perfect. I need only one. How much is it?"

"For you? Today, I will ask for one dollar." He walks back to his cash register with the rose I select and rings me up. He wraps it in clear cellophane and adds some baby's breath, small white flowers to accent the rose. "Could you take those out, please? My mom is not a fan. If you have a fern or a lemon leaf, I will take it. Otherwise, the solo rose will do," I say measuredly.

I carefully carry this rose on the long bus ride and walk the six blocks home. My only goal is to deliver it in one piece.

Over time, I came to know roses are sturdy flowers. And for me, a single flower is enough—my ritual of love.

"Disclosure" by Grandma Margaret

My face
recollects the years.
Unrealized and secret dreams
are written there without permission;
the time prints of habit,
erasing inheritance.
I search the mirror,
And find my father, my grandmother.
But you need only look at me,
To know who I really am.

CHAPTER 22

QUEST

A tree hides the sun. In the cold of the shade, cool air brings me back to the present. The events of this day fuel a desire to look at my past.

Mom's remembering makes me ready to revisit that list of names I got from Susie at BRT. I want to paint the full picture of my dad's story, not just the version I experienced.

I wrap my head around what I know. Mom and Dad returned from Greece in 1966, pregnant with me, and moved to a home in Berkeley, California, to grow their family. With the death of my grandfather, Mom received an inheritance she used to fund Dad's dream. They founded the theater in 1968 by converting a small storefront on College Avenue into a ninety-eight-seat playhouse. It was renamed the Berkeley Repertory Theatre in 1970.

Who was my dad, Michael Williams Leibert? For more than thirty-five years I've wondered, deeply, how I might understand and be like him. Being his daughter did not necessarily mean I knew him, which is a recognition that leaves me captive. What is knowing? Is it a feeling, like love? Maybe it is more like a sense of trust, that place we can go in the presence of another, that allows us to be ourselves, fully and wholeheartedly, without fear.

Most of my childhood memories surrounding my father are lonely, quiet, and sad. I don't remember any in-depth conversations between us. I've carried this vacancy without question.

At age five when my parents divorced, I lived primarily with Mom. My days were filled with worry as I was insecure and afraid most of the time. An inflated sense of responsibility grew my neuroticism and made me a stickler for punctuality. I hated to be late and still do. I created a language of love that had me overthinking every situation. Severe bronchial and digestion issues plagued my childhood. Chronic thumb sucking and nail biting followed me into my teens.

Now I am curious to find a new story, one not so distraught and limited. *What did people love about my dad? Why did they choose to work with him? What fears were challenged?*

I use the contacts Susie gave me back in 2007 to initiate my quest. I ask everyone to spread the word along with countless requests via email, phone, and handwritten letters:

> *I am seeking stories of friendship to acknowledge my dad's talent and courage as a director and an actor, to highlight his ability to bring together a group of people and spin a unique magic. Help me explore the love he generated through his relationships on*

and off stage. Some say he was a visionary. How so? Many say he changed their lives for the better and their experience with the Berkeley Repertory Theatre was never to be repeated. There appears to be strong loyalty and commitment in the theater family, remarkably so. Do I have that right?

This feels good. I'm excited and nervous. *How will people respond?* I try to let go of expectations.

I start dreaming. If I find out more about my dad, particularly the parts of him I didn't get to see growing up, I might figure out what really happened to him. Maybe I'll solve the mystery surrounding his drinking.

"Disposal" by Grandma Margaret

The Mill Valley Refuse Service truck
Grinds up yesterday
Along with the trash.
Banging his huge can at the back door,
And hoisting it to his back,
The garbage man takes my sleep, too,
Haunted with the day's happenings,
And throws it away.
The scraps and bones of last night,
The words which littered yesterday,
Are gone.
And I awake to a clean day.

CHAPTER 23

INSIGHT

It's late morning. The theme for my 9:00 a.m. yoga class was "pause with grace." The heated practice is intense. Juxtaposing the physical reality with gentle consideration is meant to enhance presence. My hope is to inspire everyone to appreciate even the hardest moments with an attitude of gratitude.

I carry this with me, sitting in my garden with a cup of my mom's favorite licorice tea. My intention is to be open to new discoveries. I hold in my hands a letter, several pages long, written by Uncle David, my dad's youngest brother.

Surrounded with the beauty I created for myself and my kids, I remember that my dad was born on April 24, 1940, to Grandma Margaret, from New York, and Grandpa Grant, from Texas. He was the first son of three boys.

I invite the generous spirits that brought me into being as I begin to read.

Dearest Meighan,

To understand Michael, you need to consider that his parents, Margaret and Grant, were introverts and highly intelligent. They were greatly influenced by the trend, popular in California at the time, that discouraged the traditional role of parents to instill values and to guide the development of the child's concepts of work ethic, religious training, etc. Therefore, in some ways, Michael was on his own and not equipped with the foundations to make appropriate decisions and exercise self-discipline. To put it bluntly, his parents failed to parent him. This does not mean he was not loved. Indeed, he was the obvious favorite of our mother and, most likely, our father too.

We had an unconventional childhood, to say the least. Whether intended or by circumstance, Michael lived most of the time with our father. Us Leibert boys were the first of our growing tribe of siblings. Our mother's personal life grew to be somewhat chaotic at times. She was busy with five children and a series of husbands. I don't know what impression this had on Michael or our brother John. I'm sure we each reacted in our own way. I can only say that I had resentments that were never vocalized, and to a large degree, I pushed them down as I tried to ignore them. I have learned I resented the lives of my friends. Being the only kid in school with divorced parents and having no curfew or required chores contributed to my not fitting in. I longed to be average, popular, and settled. It never seemed these things bothered Michael, but he was seven years older, which meant he was unlikely to confide in me if he felt the same. He was popular and handsome, which seemed to fill his world, and he was drawn to the stage early on, like a moth to a flame.

Michael excelled in sports. He was an excellent swimmer. As early as ninth grade, during his freshman year at Tamalpais High School, he had a reputation for sophistication and glamor. He would throw parties when our parents were not home that were the talk of the town. I remember cringing when my friends' mothers would comment about my wild brother or our bachelor father. Michael's pursuit of the dramatic started at an early age. He threw me in the San Rafael slough when I was three. When Mom found out, she demanded an explanation: "I wanted to see how it felt to save someone!" Sometimes he would stash me in the closet and lock the door, waiting for my terror to grow, until the shit was scared out of me, so he could come in for the rescue. He was forever the champion, the hero.

During one of Mom's dinner parties, Michael laid himself out on the driveway. He covered himself with fake blood and a butcher knife, setting the stage to shock the guests. It worked. The screams turned to laughter, eventually. One time Michael jumped off the roof of the garage while wearing a Superman cape, and he broke his leg. These behaviors earned him a reputation within the family as a talented, creative, artistic, and sensitive child. He was to be admired and given a lot of creative space. I'm not sure this served him so well. He was exalted as an exceptional person by the family, and members would gather breathlessly to hear about his latest project. He spent one summer working on the crew of a tramp steamer at age sixteen. He produced a live show at a local theater at age eighteen. These accomplishments gave him a veneer of protection when he would engage in more outrageous activities. I was the youngest of us three, and I found the whole situation puzzling.

Michael did have a kind, helpful nature as well. I recall him giving me brotherly advice that was sincere and meant to support me while navigating normal boy problems. And our childhood was far from normal. When I look back on our life together and consider my older brother, it seems to me that underneath the showman, Michael was insecure and worked diligently to hide that fact. He became a master at it—so practiced he became the public persona he presented. As an alcoholic and son of an alcoholic, it is hardly surprising that Michael would show one face to the world, hiding a deep trembling inside from fear, insecurities, and regrets. He was amazingly talented and able to uphold his façade for a long time until he simply couldn't do it anymore when the booze got the better of him.

We were not a "family of secrets," per se, but many issues and topics were not spoken about in our mother's home. In our dad's home, children were treated like adults, which essentially meant we were responsible for ourselves. I think this provided a bit of loneliness, the kind you feel when you aren't really connected with the people around you. I do not recall ever being told this or what was right or wrong or that some things just aren't morally correct. I have no idea if this approach was assumed by both parents knowingly or if it stemmed from the progressive, warped notion that kids should find their own way because parental dictates create neurosis. I know I raised myself.

I wish I could provide more insight into what motivated my brother and what dreams he carried. He did not confide in me, and I often felt he had little regard for me or my lifestyle. He was closed off in this way. Michael seemed to want what he saw on the screen or what he read in books. He would emulate renowned artists and follow their debauched ways with excess as though it was a part of being "a creative person." This seemed to overshadow any glimpse of the "real" Michael. Over the years, things he would do or say often felt rehearsed like he was always acting and in character. He didn't feel genuine to me. I'm not saying he was shallow. It was more that he was living in a pretend world, one of fantasy, and he liked it that way. I think he considered himself a sort of male version of "Auntie Mame" and people were attracted to him for that reason. I'm sure a lot more was under that façade. Unfortunately, I never got to see it.

I reread it again and again. I am not prepared for the beautiful impact his story delivers. The treasures imbedded in this heartfelt missive are eye opening. "He was the obvious favorite," "Michael was insecure and worked diligently to hide that fact," "I know I raised myself," "Michael seemed to want what he saw on the screen or what he read in books… this seemed to overshadow any glimpse of the 'real' Michael," "He was living in a pretend world."

It seems my dad and I are more alike than not. Already in my fifties, I see what confused me as a child, how my dad's unavailability maybe had nothing to do with me. Did growing up with no limits give my dad a sense of invincibility?

I chew on this as I'm brought back to reality with a call from my son's school principal. She wants to meet with both of us later today.

"Prelude and Coda" by Grandma Margaret

A solitary fly, late straggler from summer,
Buzzes in the quiet air.
The trees stand dark and naked
on their drifting, yellow leaves.
November abides.
Its' midday's warmth is stored in my buried bulbs;
It's freezing dawns and twilights
ripen the walnuts in the orchard.
From bare limbs
Sap ebbs slowly to the roots;
For the winter land is warm within.
And the pale shoots of spring
Lie safely hidden
from the chill dark wind above.

CHAPTER 24

BORING AF

"Hello, Sebastian, Mrs. Leibert. I'm so sorry," she says in the waiting room and gestures us to follow her back to her office.

"Sorry?" I laugh lightly, realizing it might be considered rude. I finish my thought anyway. "For what? My son is thrilled," I reply. Not having to go to school is a dream come true. I'm irritated with having to be here and feeling inconvenienced. Sebastian and I take our seats opposite her desk.

"Well," she says sitting down, "his insolence is a problem. Writing 'Boring AF' on the office wall during detention is bold and daring. We do not tolerate this kind of behavior. His teacher will join us momentarily. We need to have a discussion."

My eyes scan the room, finding photos of young people, perhaps her family. Framed awards and certificates cover the walls and bookshelves. A walkie-talkie sits on her desk, and I am facing the backside of two computer screens. This looks like a serious operation.

Sebastian is sitting next to me. I gently place my hand on his knee and give it a little squeeze. We spoke earlier in the car about what might happen. My frustration at being called into the school influenced my listening, making what he had to say seem hollow and inferior. My attitude changes as I engage the man responsible for the probable expulsion.

Mr. Granger enters the room ten minutes late. Dead eyes barely meet mine, giving me a strange impression. *Oh brother*, I think, *another disinterested teacher. Perfect.*

"You know, I believe Sebastian to be a bright boy," he says in a condescending tone, making me believe he is a liar.

"His rudeness and inability to control himself is a problem," Mr. Granger continues as my defenses trip. "He needs to obey my rules. I send him to the office or have him sit outside my class whenever I cannot get through to him." He's talking with his head down, as if he is speaking to the floor. I keep following his gaze to help him dig that hole.

Mr. Granger looks up at me and continues, "When I ask Sebastian to do something, he is quick to talk back. If I reprimand him for misbehavior, he always has an explanation ready. Honestly, Mrs. Leibert, I don't want to hear it." He is defensive.

That's it. He said it, the words I know all too well: *I don't want to hear it.* I am aware of what this man describes, and I am embarrassed for both of us. Why do we not want to listen to what these kids have to say?

I stay quiet to gather my thoughts. He sounds stuck, committed to his way—another familiarity. *Are we here for my son or you?*

"I'm not married," I add lightly, not caring if it throws anyone off. Mr. Granger looks at me and apologizes with a half-smile.

His argument sounds rehearsed, and his frustration clearly comes from his inability to control my son. *I know the feeling.* Seeing myself in this man is a reflection I don't like, and I am motivated to find a new way of relating with Sebastian.

He clearly is not interested in understanding my son, which makes me not like him. Where is the inquiry? What does my son find boring? Suddenly, I find myself sitting in a small box without any intention to share learning. I thought we were all here for a discussion, but instead, my son and I are on the receiving end of a reprimand.

Sebastian keeps telling me how much he dreads this class, how Mr. Granger has it out for him before he even sits down. "He hates me, Ma," Sebastian tells me repeatedly. "I know the material and want to help the other kids in class. Everything I do upsets him. It's like he doesn't want me there."

Mr. Granger's attitude helps me find my footing. With his help, my position becomes crystal clear. I am not only an advocate, but I am also a loving parent. I walked into this meeting assuming Sebastian was in the wrong, making me irritable. Sebastian's being in trouble made me think maybe I was at fault too, a painful admission.

I am now fortified by the realization my son is being unfairly accused. Even if I am mistaken, I have an opportunity to show my son I am on his side. This clarity breeds conviction to infuse me with a much-needed dose of confidence.

Sebastian will stay home for one week to review his actions.

Although I kept my mouth shut in the principal's office, the floodgates are wide open in the car. "We are not going to win this one," I tell my son. "You just have to make it to the end of the year." *Who doesn't love direction?* I think of his arrowhead. "Mr. Granger currently holds all the power, but I need you to understand that I have your back. I trust you to decide for yourself in every moment. If you need to break his rules because it doesn't sit right with you, do it, and own it. Take the hit, get sent to the hall, the office, or wherever. Hold your ground. I love you, and we will get through this."

Sebastian sits back in his seat and raises his hand to high-five me. We smack our palms together. The clap reverberates through the car. *Yes! We got this.*

My definition of family, the one that works for me, is a system that shares the responsibility of supporting its members emotionally, spiritually, and physically.

When we are held by a group of people in a way we don't like, it can feel extremely challenging to break free. My work as a mom is to notice when I am squeezing too tightly with an idea that may not actually be serving the collective. It's easy for me to slip into a place of control, usually stemming from habit and fear. As I grow my own flexibility, my kids get the space to discover for themselves.

Uncle David's letter gave me a glimpse of how my dad was raised, and I am curious what patterns of behavior I inherited. A moment from my childhood surfaces, a time when my mom couldn't see what was going on with me. *How often does that happen with my own kids?*

"Untitled" by Grandma Margaret

Poets, without words,
Write their poems in living.
And bring them forth, with love,
in every daily interaction.
They shine in all the corners of life;
Bridge the changing spaces
between seen and unseen.
In consciousness,
they watch, and listen, and respond;
And we feel their lives around us,
as we feel warmth, or hunger.
Poets, even without words,
Unite us with the world.

CHAPTER 25

LATCH KEY (MEMORY)

"Move," he says. But I don't hear him. The last bell just rang, which gives me about three minutes to get to my bus. I'm hot and preoccupied with a hole on the front of my shirt, unclear as to how it got there and feeling embarrassed about it.

"Hey, you." Now I hear him. He taps me on the shoulder. I turn around. He's a little older than me, with dark hair and brown eyes. He is plain looking. I don't know him. Hell, I don't know anybody. It's a new school, far away from home, with a gazillion students.

"What?" I respond. *Wham!* I get slugged in the stomach. I bend over and swallow the "ouch" I really want to scream. But I have no breath. Everything stops. Then he hits me again with the tire of his bike. It slams into my leg, and I fall to the ground. My backpack is heavy, pushing me into the cement. My cheek is pressed hard against cold gray pavement. I close my eyes and squeeze them. *Fuck.*

I blink my eyes open a thin sliver to watch wheels with neighboring red sneakers walk past. *I hate this school and my life.*

My bladder releases and the warmth spreads to the tops of my thighs. Clenching my jaw to hold back tears, I peel myself off the cement and reorient to standing. *I just need to get on the bus and go home.* I slide my denim jacket off my back and wrap it around my middle to hide what feels like an obvious soaking. Other kids are around, but nobody says anything. Their veiled stares surround me like an audience.

I limp onto the bus. I wonder if I smell. *I wish I were dead.* Sitting alone, I look down at my hands the entire bus ride home. They are ugly, gnawed digits. I chew my nails and suck my thumb to ease tension. My stomach still hurts. I wonder if it is bruised. It burns through my skin.

When I get home, I stand on the stoop fishing for the key around my neck. I can't get it in the lock fast enough. My bladder responds to my standing on the doormat. Like clockwork, I pee my pants for the second time today. My eyes well up with tears. I bite my lower lip hard and turn the key to open the door.

I walk immediately to the bathroom and fill the tub with water. I empty what remains of the Mr. Bubble container into the tub. He looks happy; maybe it will help. I soak my clothes and myself. I scrub long and hard, hoping to rid my skin of the afterschool memories. *What if it happens again?*

Stepping out of the floating garments, I dry myself and get dressed. Returning to the tub, I pull the plug. Once the water recedes, I wring my clothes and roll them in my towel. I carry the big terry cloth burrito to the deck and hang everything outside to dry.

Waiting for Mom to come home, I busy myself in her closet. I slide my small feet into a pair of her heels. My new height makes me feel special. I slip myself into one of her blouses, and it falls to my knees. The sheer black with gold, sparkly woven thread feels soft and silky. I see myself in the long mirror. I feel pretty with my mom wrapped around me. Her earthy sweetness floats through the air, soothing my sadness.

I lift the shirt, eyeing the dark purple gray of the bruise spreading like spilled paint across my middle. I take Mom's silk blue scarf and wrap it around my body like a bandage. I see my green eyes looking back at me with innocent admiration.

I don't know how long I was there not hearing her.

I blink, and there she is, surprising me with a glare. "Hi, Mom," I say softly.

"Meighan, what are you doing? Those are my clothes. Please put them back where you found them. Stop trying to copy me. Be yourself," she says with irritation. Her words sting.

Slowly, my small feet slide out of her shoes. I unwind myself from my blue bandage and pull her blouse off my body. I return everything to its place with care. Being exposed makes me unsure and alone. The tears begin to flow. I can't stop them. That's when the coughing starts. It's deep and hoarse and gravelly. Thrown into a bronchial tizzy, I stay home from school the next day.

"What am I supposed to do with you?" she says. *Let me stay home forever*, I answer silently.

Her words cut through me like icy wind and break me apart. *Why can't she understand how much I hate that school?*

"April 24, 1971" by Grandma Margaret

People possess the street
with their presence, their passion.
Marching feet, and flying hair,
Faces, bodies,
blurred into one body,
Have swallowed up the boulevard.
Humanity displaces
the cars and concrete it creates
To make something else;
A cry for peace.
A stride away from war.
In the sharp April wind,
Against an even sharper sword,
They become
A congregation of spirits;
A concentrated act of protest,
brotherhood, and love.

CHAPTER 26

ONCE UPON A TIME

Sitting with this memory brings up a lot of strange feelings. *Do I parent the same way? Am I too busy and distracted to see them?*

I'm reminded of the therapist who came to our home and gave me permission to let my children relax so they could decompress. Taking time to appreciate what is happening with my preteens is not an automatic response. I seem more connected to what they should be doing and how their choices will translate to the outside world, which embarrasses me to admit.

What I suffered from most as a child was feeling alone and unloved. Standing by my kids, listening to them, and attempting to understand where they are coming from will help them feel loved. I am encouraged solely by my own desire. If I can generate it, maybe I too can share in the experience of it.

I speak with Karen Ingenthron over the phone, someone who knew my father way back when. She received her bachelor of arts from UC Berkeley and was in the first production of *Woyzeck* at the BRT in 1968. She was a company member for ten years.

Her voice is warm and soft with inspirational tones of love. Her remembrance of my dad is unlike anything I could have imagined. She speaks of a man dedicated to his craft. I am mesmerized.

Because I didn't take any notes during our first conversation, Karen sent me an email to help me revisit some of the theater's beginnings.

Dear Meighan,

What an honor to be invited to write about your father, an amazing, complex human being. This courageous step of yours opened my heart to the formative, determining years of my life presided over by none other than Michael Leibert. He influenced me hugely and changed my life during the time he loved the BRT into existence. No doubt other contributors will find something unique to tell you about him, but at root they will all say the same thing that just seconds after meeting him, they felt his warmth and humanity.

How did I know him? "Once upon a time..." is what it seems like now. "I knew a remarkable person..."

We met as students excited about theater at UC Berkeley's Drama Department, each of us passionate in our desire to make theater that spoke to the human condition. Michael was a student in the directors' program while I was studying acting.

Flash: 1967. Michael hailing me as I walked away from the department office. What did he want, that older fellow who always dressed like an ivy leaguer? He aimed his eyes right at mine. Was he coming on to me? His eyes were so beautiful. What the hell color were they? No. He wanted my attention, and he wanted me to say yes. Would I be in his thesis production of *The Prodigal*? A grad student of his stature needed my skills! I said yes, and in return, got "the smile"—guileless, appreciative, joyful and inclusive.

Flash: The shower curtain "scandal." Your father was a principled man and marched the "John Lewis" path via the plethora of meaningful plays he produced. By the late 1960s protests were a daily occurrence, and everywhere students banded together to fight the injustices around them. Enter Michael Leibert, a grad student earmarked for a feather in the drama department's cap. He and I started our yearslong relationship immersed in an antiwar play, *The Prodigal*, a modern version of an ancient Greek tale that also served the moment as an antiwar statement. Michael chose this play as his master's thesis production to make a stand about the current conflict. Unlike other grad students who found set designers to work with, Michael engaged an artist. To suggest both ancient and modern elements, they devised a ceiling-to-floor wall of light, encased in plastic sheeting. The effect was stunning and 1967-ultra-modern. It evoked, depending on your take, a Southwestern aurora borealis, a sci-fi public bath house, or abstract Greek columns that surged earth tones. It was hard to find the entrances and exits in the flow of the curtain, but after navigating it like a fun house, we mastered it. It was quickly dubbed the "shower curtain set" and became the talk of the campus and irritant of drama professors!

Flash: 1968. Michael finding and saving me. While I was honored to be part of ACT's acting company right out of college, my life there during Bill Ball's drug-ridden reign devolved into tortuous disappointment. I couldn't wait to leave and couldn't afford to quit. Enter Michael, who'd gotten word of my misery. Would I audition for his new company? *New company?* Joe Spano and I auditioned on the same afternoon and were hired for the first season. It's hard without recalling the political environment and the raw details of the theater building on College Avenue, in contrast to the opulence I'd just disavowed at ACT, to express the excitement of being part of a company that felt honest and real.

The news of Michael's professional troupe was a siren call for talented artists capable of building a ten-thousand-dollar set (or costumes) for ninety-nine dollars and ninety-five cents. They showed up itching to begin Michael's new venture. What would it take? Would we succeed? It felt like an unorthodox religious calling that demanded respect and dedication. I was essentially an acolyte in Michael's playpen/ sandbox cathedral.

Michael was a magnet for his crucible on College Avenue. (Were we alchemists?) He threw dross into it; we sweated and moaned, cheered and stomped until we pounded out "pure gold!" which was your dad's ultimate thumbs-up. He told us frequently and sincerely that it was a privilege to direct us, which we always teased him about. But your dad's humility was truly awesome.

Flash: Michael Renner and I had just performed a poetry selection as a fundraiser at the Presbyterian Church on College Avenue. Your dad and theater history professor Dunbar Ogdon stood side by side, eating from dinky paper plates at the refreshments table, cordially playing a mind game. "What do you want on your tombstone?" Dunbar asked Michael. He inhaled and said, "Here lies a craftsman." Dunbar was deeply impressed. I, at age twenty-eight, thought, *That's it? Nothing else?* Now I recognize the rare humility of his response. Michael Leibert was, in essence, humble and, ironically, a craftsman of great note. What a rare and beautiful thing.

Michael wasn't even thirty when he took on that mantle of responsibility and a wife, two kids, and a dog. On any day he might direct, produce, perform, or all of the above. I don't know how he did it. He was steady, solid, and a natural peacemaker and diplomat. I cannot recall one moment of anger. Of course, that had its drawbacks. But he hated confrontation and had developed an eloquent toolbox to avoid it: encouragement, negotiation, mediation, humor, serenity, and cajoling, among others. Did I mention shoulder shrugs or food? Diplomatic white lies? In this regard, he was truly a gentleman-employer.

Flash: a lively holiday dinner party spread out on tables across the theater (on the stage). Michael called out a cheery welcome from where the richest dishes were laid out, the ones he'd made! Your dad knew a special dinner would help us manage the sacrifice of working on a holiday. In this atmosphere, his spirit was elevated and made manifest, paradoxically, as the People's Patrician, serving the spiritual family clustered around him. I remember seeing you on such occasions, which made him so happy.

Your father naturally promoted togetherness and the collective values of an ensemble—a company working together for the benefit of the whole. The opportunity to build an ensemble fueled our idealism, enthusiasm, and loyalty. Unity, a core aspect your father's personality, made working under his direction a pleasure. When he gave notes, they were framed in the positive: "do this" rather than "don't do that." You felt he was on your side. He was an actor, too, and wasn't going to pull rank, humiliate you, or apply undue pressure. He patiently allowed his cast to make their own discoveries, a gift for actors. Michael praised his workers (cast and crews), and the sincerity of it made everyone feel secure.

Your dad had more than a wee bit of Irish magic about him. He had the ability to bring talent together and the foresight to let them create without blocking their growth with micromanagement. He had little to offer in the way of salary or fancy resources. For those who understood his philosophy of theater (that the performance communicates the truth), it was an exciting challenge, a thrill, a calling to make something out of nothing. Those who got it bonded in joy.

The feeling of connection between the actors and the audience was a surprise result of the authenticity of our work. There may have been finer actors in the world, much better sets, etc., but our sincerity and devotion were unquestioned.

Love,
Karen

I lean back and reflect. My dad built his life in theater. What must it have felt like for him to know so young? Where's my talented calling?

Face it, Meighan. That just isn't your story, I think. Maybe I'm just not looking at it in the right way. A broad smile spreads across my face as I add, *You are just beginning.*

I like the words "sincerity and devotion"—character-building qualities not present in our father-daughter relationship growing up. Dad wasn't at home with us because he was busy with his other family. I imagine the thrill and joy of building a dream, especially with the backdrop of the Vietnam War. The positive and nourishing connection of a family breeds hope. Creative expression is a powerful tool for communication, and now I see my dad as a pioneer, committed to his cause—one that did not include me.

Insecurity plagued my childhood. "Sincere praise" was not something I experienced. I learned from the letter Uncle David wrote that my dad was a master at hiding his own insecurities. How did he become a conduit of strength for those around him and not for me? It appears to be so natural for him, like he was meant to do it.

Feeling into Karen's words brings back a memory from my childhood—a time when Dad did not choose me.

"Nocturne" by Grandma Margaret

Now is the silent core of night,
Still as a snowfall,
Quiet as peace;
Death still, so I can plainly hear
The slight nocturnal sounds of life.
Faintly the metronomes of breath
Measure unconscious passing hours
Of dreams, forgotten with the light,
Of shapes and scenes unknown by day.
A hand is flung against the wall,
My child half speaks, her words unclear.
And then I hear a click of claws,
The watchful cat prowls past my door.
Outside, no cars drive by the house,
No people pass,
No sound breaks through
This almost total, crowded silence,
Breathing, moving, and alive.

CHAPTER 27

BUTTER (MEMORY)

FIVE YEARS OLD

Saturday delivers lazy mornings. The coffee table, covered with drawings and colored pencils, has been keeping me busy for the past hour.

Eavesdropping outside the kitchen, I pause before I make my move. I've been ready for an hour, waiting for him to pick me up. We are going to the zoo.

Behind me is the living room framed with a wall of windows overlooking the bay. It's like living in a painting that changes every day. The sky determines the mood. Today is gray and the clouds are heavy in the sky, but there is no fog. The white sails of boats dart through the water. They blur together when I watch for too long, and my eyes get tired.

Mom is in the kitchen. I hear her crying and talking softly. It makes me sad.

"Where are you?" she says. It's Dad's turn, and he's not here, *again*.

"When are you coming?" I hear her ask into the phone.

I slip around the corner and keep my head down. I don't want to look straight at her, afraid she might see me.

"She's so excited," I hear Mom say.

A round table sits near the entrance with three chairs. I rest my small left hand on its edge as I raise my eyes to look along the surface of the countertop. I see the royal blue butter dish next to the glass salt-and-pepper shakers. Raising my right arm to reach for it, I stand on my tiptoes to make contact. I pull it toward me and turn to face the table with my body.

Mom spins to her right, facing the refrigerator, keeping me out of sight. The phone is attached to the wall near the water cooler. She's wrapped herself in the spiral white cord that travels the length of the kitchen.

Placing the butter dish on the table, I slide open the utensil drawer and pull out a small spoon. I can't tell if Mom knows I am here.

Wedging myself into the chair farthest from Mom, I lift the blue lid off the golden sweetness and place it on the table. I cut the butter with the edge of the spoon and then slip it into my mouth and let the silky-smooth texture melt over my tongue. My eyes close as I savor the experience. This is my heaven. I put another spoonful in my mouth and sit back in my chair. I swallow, following the buttery flavor down my throat.

"Depending on you is exhausting," she delivers firmly, unwinding herself from the cord and hanging up the phone. She walks out of the room before I can tell her I will be okay on my own.

Sadness grips my stomach, twisting tightly and unsettling me in my seat. Another spoonful of butter lands on my tongue as I try to ignore the pain in my belly. How many times have I watched my mom weep through his excuses, the ones that tell her repeatedly he is too busy to be a part of our lives in a meaningful way?

Why doesn't he want to see me?

"Unsuited" by Grandma Margaret

I could never be a real
Hippie.
Tramping shoeless down the road,
Or sleeping on a beach,
I'd die of cold.
Someone would find me
in the morning;
Clutching a flower,
Face to the stars,
But frozen.
She meant well, they'd say.

CHAPTER 28

DEODORANT

Joe Spano is another actor from the BRT on College Avenue. He met my dad at UC Berkeley. After he graduated, Joe spent the next ten years at Berkeley Rep. His migration to Los Angeles delivered his role as Lt. Henry Goldblume on *Hill Street Blues*. He spent ten years as the voice of Walgreens and twenty years with *NCIS* as FBI Special Agent Tobias C. Fornell. He considers himself very lucky.

Joe's friendship with my mom continues to this day.

I remember him as my first Dracula at BRT on College Avenue when I was a young girl. It sparked my obsession with vampires. I became sincerely devoted to *Creature Features* on late-night TV only to hang garlic around my bedframe and wear turtlenecks to sleep.

When I receive his email, I am immediately delighted by the title. *Here we go*, I think.

"Your Dad"
Dear Meighan,

I wrote a whole piece that I thought was smart and funny, maybe a little snarky. And then I read Bill Oliver's piece from the memorial in the Studio Theater (I think you may have sent it to me) and realized I had left out what was most important about Michael. Bill ended with it, and I am going to restart my memory with it.

Your dad was a kind man. He never, ever was mean to or belittled me, and he probably had more than enough cause, often enough, to do so.

I suppose he could be called a visionary in retrospect, but that idea would not have been part of our relationship. I insisted on relating to him as the charming, risk-taking entrepreneur he also was. I strove to see him as an equal, a fellow artist and the sometimes odd father of this strange family I had joined and come to love deeply. I took every advantage to mark, and remark on, what I saw as his foibles. It all seems so petty and unimportant now, but it was important to my finding my voice and it was important he never turned his back on me.

And I love him. I love him because he gave me room to discover and express myself. He saw, honored, and sometimes humored my ideas, indeed my very being, by creating an artistic safe house where I was able to learn a craft I have practiced for fifty-seven years. A craft that has gifted me with more than a living...a life...of creativity. A craft that has given me the greatest of joys and comforted the greatest sorrows.

I love him for employing me, when I wasn't in a show, as a waiter (and one night the chef) at Trespassers W, the restaurant he and Flicka built a few doors down from the theater. I can still see him, in his *Alchemist* costume, appearing at the rear Dutch door to delight in a glass of red wine between scenes.

And I love him and Flicka for letting me caretake Santos Ranch, the magically beautiful house they built on eighty acres of cattle-grazing, oak grassland high above Pleasanton: all-concrete domes and a soaring-wood main house with a sod roof and decks and columns from the old San Francisco Hall of Justice and chickens and ducks and a final two-day blast-goodbye to the great old days...an event nobody remembers but that everybody can recall.

I love him most tenderly for crashing, with Ron Vernan, Joan's and my wedding at the Brazilian Room in Tilden Park after I had left the theater and moved to LA. Thinking that we were done with each other and had gone to different worlds, I chose not to invite him, no doubt feeling critical personally and haughty professionally. I was, of course, wrong and unkind to be astonished by the effrontery but delighted, in the end, to be taught that we must always crash the weddings of the people we truly love.

And finally, I love that, in his traditional welcoming address to each and every new cast, he never failed to insist on the use of mouthwash and deodorant.

Reading Joe's words makes me see Dad as an amazing person—talented, fun, a great friend, with a sense of humor to boot. This gives me hope that I might be capable of it too.

Deeply moved by the love Joe has for the man I call Dad forces me to reconsider how he felt like a stranger for most of my life. As I immerse myself in the glorious details of my dad's theater life, I find a world filled with dedication, hard work, and always an opportunity to share a laugh.

This is what I've been missing. My seriousness has pushed me too far afield. I'm either scraping by on the edge or in a free fall with my eyes closed.

Ignoring my past is not an act of freedom. It is quite the opposite. Claiming my memories opens a new experience all together, one that doesn't have me feeling so alienated. Every single chapter of my life contributes to the story. If I leave one out, I miss an important message.

My dad was a good human. I want to be that too.

"North Coast" by Grandma Margaret

This is the end of the land.
This coast, strewn with flowers.
Wounded and washed by the waves,
Beaded with fog,
and trailing the soft, shrill cries of seabirds,
It holds up blossoms
that tremble sweetly in the fierce wind.
Here, the tidal water
rises to the meadows. And the river running fresh
from a
dusty valley,
Mingles with the salt inlet.
This is the edge of the continent,
A wreath from the sea.

CHAPTER 29

A RARE BREED

I asked Karen Ingenthron to spread the word of my "stories of friendship" project and receive a call from Thomas Lynch late one afternoon. We speak briefly and set a date to meet at his apartment in Berkeley. He lives across the street from the original site for the theater on College Avenue.

I park several blocks from Thomas's address and use the long walk to ease my excitement of meeting an actor, in the flesh, who knew my dad. Thomas greets me at the door with an infectious grin. I follow him into his two-room apartment to find a wall of windows facing south. A pastoral vista stands before me, bringing the beauty of trees warmed by the sun a little closer. The twinkle of birdsong hangs in the background, an audible brushstroke to complete the picture.

"My neighbor made us muffins," he tells me, gesturing for me to sit at his kitchen table.

"Thomas, thank you so much for taking the time. Being here with you means so much to me," I say genuinely.

"My dear, it is an absolute pleasure," he reassures. "Now tell me. What do you want to know?"

"I want to know why my dad drank," I admit frankly. Then I add, "Were you close? Could you be considered a confidante?"

"Ooh. Those are good questions," he says, pouring me tea. I nibble at one of the muffins as I wait. "I can tell you this: Your dad and I were close, for a long time, until he didn't want to be. I wasn't afraid to tell your dad what I thought about anything. He knew I didn't like his drinking, and eventually, it took him from me."

"Yeah," I say. "Me too. Do you have any idea what compelled him to drink? Was it stress?" I ask worriedly.

"Everybody drank back then. I mean, sure, Alcoholics Anonymous was around. But we were all young. Drinking was a big part of our lives. And some of us, like your dad, couldn't seem to get a handle on it. Maybe he was stressed. I'm not sure." Thomas pauses. I bite my tongue as I hope he's thinking. He continues, "I can tell you this. Your dad was smart and super talented, a rare breed. His vision of theater held many of us close. He lost control when the theater got bigger. With the addition of the board of directors, things got tougher. The expansion project was a dream for some, not all. But who knows?"

This shifts our conversation to focus on what we do know. We are drawn to talk about our childhoods. We uncover personal truths we've not spoken out loud to anyone. I reveal a few of my painful memories and how losing dad contributed to my misusing male attention.

Here we are, essentially strangers, united by a love for a man who marked us deeply, sharing our underbellies in the light of day.

This is meaningful to me. And I appreciate that my dad made it possible.

Spending time with Thomas is the closest I've felt to Dad since my quest began. The phrase "kindred spirits" comes to mind, and I imagine this is what Dad's company was all about: a group of people sharing their imaginations in a soul-enhancing expression of love.

Living true is exciting. That's what I hear when I read these stories from long ago. The Berkeley Repertory Theatre was special.

I say goodbye to Thomas and promise to stay in touch. My heart is full.

Thomas emails me the next morning, a poem and three recollections from his time at BRT. With my kids at school, I brew a fresh cup of coffee and prepare for a ride down memory lane.

> Hi Meighan,
> I wrote this poem today. I woke up to it and had to make it real. It reminds me a bit of our conversation, how you shared with me. I will never forget it.

"Morning Wake"

When I find the quiet of my soul
I hear music
It is soft and gentle
It draws me in and cradles me close
This is comfort
I am here to help
We all need healing
Together we can change
And together we can grow
We are one
Some of you may need to share your dark
Give it to me
When you let it out
There is more room for your light to shine through
I can receive and support your release
The magic you possess
Is a big part of your significance
Bring it forward
So we may believe
And feel your power
The beauty in you
Magnifies the beauty in me
No longer hide in pain
Set yourself free
Come play with me

MICHAEL THE STORYTELLER

A fact I'd like you to know, when he had time on his
hands, is he would just sit at his desk and edit plays.
He was not necessarily going to do them; it was just

practice. He knew how to tell a story, and he wanted to tell it as skillfully as he could. We did *Who's Happy Now*, which was in the original small round theater. At the end he had me walk out and made my clicking shoes important as I left the stage through the lobby and out the back door. The audience really couldn't see me after I left the auditorium...very powerful.

THE WILD DUCK

As a young actor I was looking at all the lead roles. I figured out I was a character actor while I was beginning my career at The Theatre on College Avenue in Berkeley. By the time we did *The Wild Duck*, I had already played several really special older guys, but Old Ekdal was to me magical. Michael was not the director of the play, but he took over eventually because he didn't approve of how it was ending (and neither did I). It was so valuable for my character, who completes the importance of dreams and love held in that area, to go into the attic at the end. I had been previously directed not to go into the attic and it was devastating for me on many levels. In short, it just didn't feel right. When Michael made that breakthrough, I remember going into the attic and just crying because it completed my function. The fact that Michael understood meant so much to me and we never even talked about it.

I had this idea that the kids should be more involved in the goings-on. I told Michael I wanted to do a children's show. He liked the idea. There was a completely untamed plot behind the theater, and Michael got the crew to clear it and build a small outdoor stage for my creation. It went quite well and as a result I named my eventual company "The Pyramus and Thisby Children's Theater."

Thomas Lynch was a BRT company member for several years in the early '70s. He left to continue The Pyramus and Thisby Children's Theater, which started at BRT. He later produced an album of his music entitled *Songs from the Elmwood* and acted locally with various equity companies, particularly Marin Shakespeare. He is currently a director for Berkeley's Actors Reading Writers.

I am reminded of the stack of books next to Dad's bed. *How do you read multiple books at the same time? Maybe it depends on your mood.*

As I go about the next few days, pieces of Thomas's email stay with me. I am reciting his memories like my own, and his words seem to add so much to the image of my father. "It was just practice...skillfully...the fact that Michael understood meant so much to me." The professional camaraderie carries the most weight. The respect and appreciation my dad gave Thomas is a beautiful expression of love.

A memory comes forward. I am twelve years old, trying to connect with my mom.

"Hedonist" by Grandma Margaret

Don't talk about it,
Do it.
Don't recommend,
But share.
Don't analyze the feeling,
Just celebrate,
and dare
To plunge into the moment,
Whatever it may say;
Nor lust for immortality,
But live, instead,
Today.

CHAPTER 30

THROWN AWAY (MEMORY)

I write a long letter to my mom, describing my feelings and current concerns. Talking with her is impossible. I only seem to enjoy her full attention when she is upset with me. Reaching her, getting her to understand me, is too hard. At least it feels that way.

It takes me a few hours. I write three different letters and finally decide to give her the one that is the truest version, filled with honest confusion and remorse rather than excuses. I tell her I'm sorry for always messing up, that I don't mean to get in her way. I only want to help, whether by taking care of my brother and sister, making breakfast and lunches, getting us off to school, or doing the laundry on weekends. All of it means something to me. I take these responsibilities seriously. But nothing I do, even when I get it right, makes either of us feel good. I explain my poor choices come mostly from trying to make friends and getting people to like me. I don't know why it's so hard, but I assure her I am doing my best. My efforts come from a good place. I promise to do better, to work harder, and to pay attention.

Maybe if she understands me, we can be closer. *This has to work.*

She's in the kitchen preparing food. I peer around the corner, and I feel the insides of my stomach start to knot. I hesitate. I hear her chopping on the cutting board. With her head down, in concentration, I see the light from the window warming her dark curls from behind. *My mom is so beautiful.*

I smell the earthy sweetness of garlic and rosemary from the kitchen doorway. I take a long slow breath in, let it out, and step into the kitchen.

I don't want to chicken out. "Mom, I wrote you a letter," I say, moving toward her. I immediately sense I am disturbing her. I stop a few feet away. I hand her the neatly folded yellow legal pad pages—my heart and soul poured out in words.

She stops chopping and turns toward me after she lays down the knife. "Meighan, what is this? I do not have time for it right now. Can't you see I am busy?" she says abruptly. It just comes shooting out of her mouth. She will not read it, and I watch my soul-infused heart-speak slip through her fingers like sand. The papers fall to the floor, and I clench my fist, promising never to do it again. Thrown away.

I walk back to my room as heat spreads across my cheeks. I cry and bend my twelve-year-old self in half, flopping on my bed. I feel rejected, and my *good intentions* were *abandoned.*

"Mendocino Beach" by Grandma Margaret

I need roots to withstand this wind.
It pulls me out, like a tide;
Out sea.
Better to lie
flat and safe against the sand.
Held down by fear,
and clutching at space,
The weight of a star
pins me to the land.

CHAPTER 31

KALEIDOSCOPE

Sebastian is in a phase of being distant and unavailable. We're not on the same page these days, making me uncomfortable because I don't like feeling out of the loop.

"Good morning, Ma," he says walking into the kitchen.

"Good morning." I smile back at him. "Veggie scramble with toast or a bagel?"

"Just the scramble," he answers.

"Don't forget we are going to Grandma's for dinner tonight. Be home by five."

"Okay, sure thing." As much as I try to relax into my son's confirmation, I have a strange sense of foreboding. I shake it off and presume I'm emotionally off kilter from reliving my dad's past and funky moments of my own. I've begun going through newspaper clippings to understand the story behind his quitting, since my gut thinks he was pushed out.

"Hey," I say giving him a glass of water. "Everything okay?"

"Yeah, Mom, I'm good," he affirms. What I hear doesn't match what I'm feeling. Something is off. I just can't put my finger on it.

Nine hours later, I get the call as I am driving into San Francisco. Frankie and I are in the car, going to family dinner without my thirteen-year-old son because he wasn't home by 5:00 p.m. I had thought about going to find him to help save face from showing up without my eldest child and decide against it. I just said, "Fuck it."

"This is Officer Thompson. May I speak with Mrs. Leibert?" I hear the voice say as my body stiffens.

"Hi, this is she," I say nervously. "My name is Meighan."

"I am with your son. We are issuing a 5150 and taking him to the emergency room," he says to me in a neutral tone. *What?* I've heard the term 5150, but I do not really know what it means.

"Is he okay? I am on my way to San Francisco. I can be there in twenty-five minutes." I feel the shock beginning to settle into my body. It is dense and solid. My spine locks, and parts of me harden.

"Your son has requested you not be here, ma'am," he says.

I repeat the words to myself in my head. I resist their meaning. I am unprepared.

"What?" Like a leaky faucet, I drip along. "Oh...really? Is he okay? What's a 5150?" I stop to inhale.

The voice on the other line begins, "He's fine." *I hate those words.* "It's a seventy-two-hour psychiatric hold. Your son, a minor, was drinking with friends on top of a roof at the middle school. We got the call from one of his friends. Your son was intent on jumping. We will have the doctors check him out, and they will decide next steps."

My head is spinning. "Do I call you or the hospital to find out what is happening?" I ask. I can no longer feel my body.

"When we get there, I will call you back with that information," he assures. I do not feel assured.

"Okay. What am I supposed to do in the meantime?" I ask desperately.

"Wait," he says in a matter-of-fact tone.

"May I speak with him?" I am trying to be calm. *Please, oh please, let me hear his voice.*

"He does not want to talk with you at the moment," he says, and my heart twists. "He's at the age when he can choose to have his parents involved or not." *What the hell?* I feel suspended, as if the floor has been removed from under my feet.

"Okay. Thank you, Officer. Goodbye." The anger I feel is confusing. Helplessness tickles the back of my throat. *Why is this happening?*

"Don't worry, ma'am. He is in good hands. We will take good care of him. I will call you back soon. Goodbye." I hang up the phone and grip the steering wheel. Then I scream, "Oh god. Frankie. What the fuck is happening!"

My whole body wants to turn the car around and drive to the ER, but I resist. Frankie is already furious. I can feel it. She is angry I do not go to the hospital or try harder to fix it. She keeps repeating, "Mom, turn around now."

"Francesca," I say a little too loud. "Please. I can't. I won't. And it's super hard for me." She crosses her arms and slumps in her seat. *God, how I wish I were her age and somebody else was driving.* Vespa senses the tension and puts her paws between us on the center console.

Scanning my body keeps me busy. I don't feel like crying. Fear has me wound tightly. I am absolutely bewildered and surprised, maybe numb. Not in a million years would I have imagined this happening. *Sebastian wants to kill himself?*

I continue to move forward to my mom's house, driving through what feels like an emotional haze. Full of resistance and dread, I take my youngest child and my dog into an old familiar, to be with family while I sit in the eye of the storm.

After telling them the news, the wave washes over me. I am surrounded by a kaleidoscope of worry and concern. The crimson reds of judgment and disbelief are followed with the dead purples of opinions and criticism. I listen and do not let the colorful words sway me. I do not agree with any of it, giving me the opportunity to shed layers of an old identity. I am less attached to my victim attitude. I know what we need.

More important, I know how to trust myself even when I'm scared.

Standing in my mom's kitchen, I am not sure what to say and keep my mouth shut. I walk into another room and call a friend who might be able to explain what is happening.

"Hi," I say. "Sebastian just got picked up by the police. They are issuing a 5150." I jump right in; no need to skirt the truth.

My shock at hearing my words immediately delivers something I don't like. It makes me swirl. I want to run and I also want to stay.

"I am so sorry, Meighan," my friend tells me. "It is so intensely scary. I've been through three of these. My best advice? Relax and let go. He's safe. Use this time to rest. Wait for them to call you."

"Really? All I want to do is get in my car and go to the hospital. But he doesn't want me there," I whine.

"No," she affirms. "There is nothing you can do. It is totally out of your hands. This is your window to recharge. I will call you tomorrow with all the programs I recommend for when he gets out. You got this!"

"Okay, thanks," I say, wanting only to crawl into bed and hide from the world. *How do I make this nightmare go away?* I still do not know what is really happening other than my son is unreachable. The pain of not knowing hits hard.

I need to trust what is here.

I'm scared, plain and simple. Placing my hand on my daughter's angry shoulder, I feel her eyes imploring me to rescue him. Then she lends voice to her thoughts and tells me outright, "You always fix it, so do it now. You can't leave him there alone."

The truth burns. I lean in and taste the strands of her long blond hair tickle my lips as I whisper, "He does not want to see me. And as much as I want to be there for him, I need to stay here for me."

The confusion I suffer, listening to my family and wondering about my son, forces me to reroute myself. I cannot hold both. Drowning in the heartfelt waters, poured from the language of love I knew as a child, I choose to swim in a different direction.

I hear my internal voice declare, "No more." Inspired and driven by hope, intuition calls me forward and I find clarity. Here I draw a line. On the far side I write "yours," on the side closest is "mine." Emboldened, I find the strength to separate myself out from what used to drag me down.

Frankie and I leave my mom's house after a few hours. I have a strong realization that I am standing on a precipice, facing the great unknown, and I am ready to wait for Sebastian to come forward. My son is in crisis, and communication is on his terms. *Do I choose to feel helpless or empowered?*

The next morning, I get a call from Sebastian's doctor. He phones as I am trying to decide if I want to go to a yoga class. I welcome his attention and stay put.

"Mrs. Leibert, this is Dr. Andersen. Your son is in my care," he says in a low voice.

"Hi, Dr. Andersen. I'm glad to hear from you," I say honestly.

"Sebastian is doing well," he says. I relax a bit after hearing this. "It seems he had a major depressive disorder episode triggered by an event. I've been working with him over the past few days. He's a wonderful kid, open and forthcoming. It makes my job a lot easier when I have a patient willing to participate."

"Were you able to determine the trigger?" I ask, eager to find out if I did something to push my son over the edge.

"Yes, I think we did, but it's confidential. He would be the one to tell you."

"I understand," I lie. But I can't help myself. I need to know more. "How is he doing? Will he need medication? Does he get to come home soon? How do we know what he needs?" I'm a little embarrassed.

"We will know more in a few days," he assures me. "Medication is a possibility. How he responds to it is the main issue."

I immediately imagine antidepressants. Dr. Andersen then adds, "Education will be valuable. We will start that here in treatment—coping skills, being comfortable talking about what is happening when it shows up."

"Are there programs for parents too, to help me know how to support him?" I ask.

"Yes. Dialectical behavioral therapy is a great place to start," he suggests. I write it down immediately. "It is a system for helping individuals understand and accept their intense and often difficult feelings. We will provide you with resources when he is discharged. For now, trust we are taking good care of your son and giving him the support he needs." *I want to, with all my heart. This is fucking hard!*

Dr. Andersen tells me I can call him to check in on Sebastian's progress and gives me his office hours. After we hang up, I spend an hour researching DBT online.

Being with myself while wanting to be with him is suffocating. I can't find my breath. A part of me seems to be missing, like a limb or an internal organ. As I sit with this, I discover a truth I am slow to acknowledge—my talent for distancing myself through superficial tasks.

What am I resisting?

Frankie and I go on with our days amid the vacancy of not knowing anything about what Sebastian is going through. My imagination is unfriendly.

Driving home from work one night, overwhelmed with my son's absence, I begin to count. He's been gone four days—ninety-six hours, 5,760 minutes, 345,600 seconds. Obsessing over what is not here is an old song I thought I'd forgotten.

Part of me is relieved he is safe and under the care of professionals, but not being able to speak with him, to hear his voice or see him, is unbelievably challenging. I want to sleep with my eyes open, so I'm ready.

"Quest" by Grandma Margaret

"Give me your love," you said
and didn't mean it.
So lightly said,
yet heard with fife and drums;
Like words of fire, or long remembered music,
still interrupting sleep
like pain—or dreams.
For what you asked I had already given.
Lavish, improvident gift
bestowed too soon.
And, now, bereft,
without your even knowing,
I seek my wandering, once incorporate, heart.

CHAPTER 32

TO THE MOON AND BACK

I begin collecting notes from friends and family and put together a small bag of clothes. I give Sebastian one personal reminder of his strength and the love that surrounds him. I enclose the letter I wrote to celebrate his marking ceremony after his camping trip with a group of boys/men a month ago—a rite of passage.

Marking Ceremony, July 17, 2020

Sebastian, I have watched you grow for the past thirteen years, witnessed your many pivots with sincere wonder and occasional irritation.

As a family we have already experienced so much. And now, we are living in the world of COVID-19.

I am truly amazed at the steadfast grace and calm you have exhibited these past few months. You have become a strong individual and a dependable team player. Your awareness has expanded. We are now experiencing your humor, generosity, true sense of personal responsibility, absolute willingness to participate, and the real physical reality surrounding your height. I do not believe I ever considered looking *up* to you.

As you already know, your spirit animal is the grizzly bear. This totem is a symbol of freedom, strength, and understanding. These qualities fuel our connection as we develop respect and kindness for each other. Although we may not agree or even like what is happening in any given moment, we always hold appreciation between us. I admire your sensitivity and wholeheartedness. Your ability to self-regulate has been slow coming, and I now fully support your reclusive nature, the aspect that calls you to pull back from activities that drain your energy. You are also magnetic, a charmer, and a wonderful traveling companion. Your interest in new things and other people's stories activate your leadership skills. You have an inner knowing I experience daily.

As I provide you the space to explore and exercise your true nature, authenticity seems to bubble up in full force. When it comes to parenting, I am choosing to follow my heart. Resisting the deeply ingrained notion to fit you into a box has been the best conscious action I have ever taken.

Today we are here to recognize the boy you were and the man you are becoming. I will keep it simple. We are so lucky to have you with us. You are a special human with a great capacity to engage and deliver.

Thank you for your curiosity and for saying yes to my many suggestions even though you think some of them are crazy ideas.

Together we are stronger.
I love you to the moon and back, foreverly, Mom

The hospital is an hour drive north. I take Vespa with me and hope I remember to breathe. I have no expectations other than the small hope I will get to see him.

It feels like a prison with an intercom for entry and glass partition at the front desk. Everything is happening behind closed doors. Even the air feels dull and heavy. The only person I meet is the nurse who comes to check the bag to make sure nothing dangerous is inside.

"Do you know my son?" I beg.

"What's his name?" she asks.

"Sebastian," I say. "He is tall, skinny, with brown hair, gray eyes, and a wicked sense of humor. He is charming and polite, eager to engage."

"Yes. He seems like a good kid. He's doing well," she says.

Suddenly, my heart beats. This news is helpful. "Oh, thanks so much. That makes me feel better," I say.

When I get to the car I break down and cry for the first time since this all happened. "We're going to be okay, Vespa," I say into her ear. We just have to stay the course.

My days seem to never end. Every minute feels like a day. My body is on high alert, fully charged and unable to calm down. The unknown is a vacuous place, especially when it involves my child.

Driving home one afternoon, my phone rings. I do not recognize the number. *Maybe it is the hospital.*

"Hello, this is Meighan," I answer hopefully.

"Hi, Ma," Sebastian says. These words, his voice—they are music. My whole being opens to wrap him in my arms through the Bluetooth.

"Oh my god!" I screech. "Sebastian. Hi, hi, hi. Sweet boy! How are you?" I am happily surprised. Eager to listen, I try to remind myself to shut up. My exuberance is ridiculous, but it seems I've found air after being without it for so long.

I pull over to park. The Golden Gate Bridge stands majestically in its orange-red color with a backdrop of a steel blue sky. Under the shade of a cypress tree, I look out to the bay and watch the boats go by, steadfast with direction.

Without knowing where we are headed, I focus on the fact he phoned me. Here we are, sailing through in our own way.

I give Sebastian my full attention, flooded with excitement. I try to slow down because I desperately want to follow his lead.

"Hi, Mom. I'm doing okay. How are you? I'm so, so sorry," he starts. His voice sounds so good. I sense regret with a hint of confidence too. *Is that possible?*

Tears brim my eyes as I attempt to focus my breathing. I want to inhale him through the phone. By slowing myself down, I allow just enough space for all that he is holding to rush out. It comes fast and furiously. I close my eyes to concentrate.

"Mom," he starts. "I didn't want to see you because I wasn't ready. I was afraid. I thought you'd get mad. When I was in the ambulance, I asked them how much it would cost. I didn't want to make things harder for you. I promise. My mess, Ma. I got super lost and started to feel really bad, like maybe it just wouldn't matter. I drank too much. Maybe jumping would make it easier—Dad leaving, moving to South America without saying goodbye. Maybe it's all my fault. I don't know how to handle wanting to love someone who doesn't want to love me back. And when I got here, they told me I could decide for myself if I wanted you with me. Then I felt bad all over again in a different way. How would I face you? Then figured I could use the space to see for myself who I am, you know, without you. I'm really sorry, Mom. I've missed you so much. And this place is really intense. I like my doctor a lot. "

I choke on his words, dry and chalky, like liquid sand. The truth is revealed. Here I thought I was his rock, only to find out he is his own. I recognize his fortitude, his courage, his bravery.

The gift is delivered in a torrential swoop. *Who am I without you?*

"Ma," he says, "are you mad?" I sense concern.

"Sebastian, how can I be mad? From what I understand, you couldn't help it. The doctor says you had a major depressive disorder moment. Something in you snapped, and you went dark. Does that sound familiar? Has he spoken to you about it? Are you mad?" I immediately regret flooding him with questions.

"I guess," he says. I can hear him thinking. "I was feeling pretty low. That's for sure. I was mad, furious actually, but I don't feel it anymore." He says this last bit with a strength that surprises me.

I wonder if they will release him in a few days or if he will need to stay longer. I'm afraid to ask for details, but I do it anyway. "Do you know what caused it? Do you remember any of what you were thinking about?"

"Dad," he answers in a flat tone. I detect no emotion.

"Yeah?" I offer gently, with a hint of curiosity.

"I was stuck on thinking how he could move to South America without saying goodbye," he tells me. My heart sinks. I prepare myself for more. "It just makes me think he doesn't care about me at all," he says sadly. "He acts like I don't exist. At first it pissed me off, and I got angry. And then I started thinking about those times when Dad was super mean. It sucked."

"Yeah," I say again. "Oh, Sebastian. This is so hard, and I am here *with* you, for as long as you'll have me. I can't speak for your dad. And I can tell you this: His leaving was about him, not you."

Then I decide to be honest—share something, take a risk, and see how it lands. "Sebastian, I know this might sound crazy, but I think I need to thank you."

"Thank me? Mom, that *is* totally crazy," he says with a laugh. *Oh, how I wish I could see you!*

"Well, this is what you do, and I am grateful for it. You turn shit upside down so we can see clearly. You did it two years ago when you reported the abuse, and now you are doing it again by telling us the truth of what's going on with you. Your courage inspires. It invites us all to change. We are lucky!"

"Mom, I should be thanking you." He sounds embarrassed, unable to wrap his thirteen-year-old brain around me *appreciating* his falling apart. I go on to explain that once again he championed this family, catapulted us wide-eyed into an arena that would forever change us for the better, where we learn to love, hear, care for, and hold each other with new depth and wonder.

Somewhere within this exchange I realize I will never be able to keep my son from taking his life if it is something he wants for himself. Letting him go is an act of love. It is best for me to appreciate him fully now and show him how much I value his presence.

"Ma, I have to go. Somebody else wants to use the phone. But before I do, I want to tell you something: I love you to the moon and back." This is a saying he delivered several years ago, defining the length of what holds us together. "Immeasurable" comes to mind, infinite. I receive his words, and my temperature rises.

He continues, "I'll call again soon. I promise. Sorry I waited so long. I miss talking with you. But I think I needed to get my head on straight, you know?" I sense a smile on the other end of the line.

"Yes. I get it, Sebastian. I am super proud of you. I love you tons!" I say, sending him my heart.

On my drive home, my relief is expansive. I may not know what is coming, but right now, I am okay. *We are connected.*

Outside our bubble I get messages of fear and judgment. I have people in my life who are angry with me because I refuse to punish my son. I am threatened with the likelihood of it happening again if I don't do something to prevent it. Others consider him to be seeking attention and add that suicide is a coward's way out. Some are bold, criticizing him for stressing our family when we are strapped keeping our businesses alive during a global pandemic. These painful reactions are a hard reminder. Delusional exists. I choose to only focus on my triad.

Sebastian comes home after a week in the care facility. We persevere. The three of us start therapy, a range of modalities, for months, alone and together. This is not graceful or fluid. It is quite choppy and bumpy. We are expressive. We have tough conversations. Sebastian tries medication, but it makes everything worse. I watch my son spiral. He adopts a list of coping skills to fit any situation. We are desperate at times, and we stay close through all of it. Self-regulation is a daily practice.

I learn to sit beside my son while giving him room to grow. My orca medicine tells me this is my place.

Alcohol is just another secret. It took my dad, so maybe it took my husband too. My son turned to it when he was in crisis. My mom always told me growing up, "It is important to know your relationship with booze. Make it your friend, not your enemy. Use it, like any drug, as a tool."

I didn't know how to do that. I abused alcohol for years. It started in high school. My self-destructive behavior lasted decades, an unconscious commitment to punishing myself.

My mom's words mean something to me today, at the young age of fifty-three. This must be a sign I am growing up, shifting from that place of feeling stuck. I am flooded with disappointment as I remember being close to Sebastian's age at a time when I needed my dad.

"Garden Harpies" by Grandma Margaret

Nasturtiums shriek orange,
Switch their tails,
And stick out their dark red tongues,
Like lily pads,
their leaves draw serene circles
around them,
and try not to notice.

CHAPTER 33

WILTED FLOWER

Father-Daughter Tea is an annual school event. We're only thirty minutes late when I find him downstairs in the empty cafeteria, draped in a chair. He appears unstructured, so I stand close, worried he might slip.

"Dad? What's wrong with you?" I ask stupidly. My naive fourteen-year-old brain expects him to answer. Clenched fists hang at my side like weights. Fingernails pierce the skin of my palms as I consider my options. With tight shoulders and a hard knocking in my chest, I hold his hand. *I'll just pretend everything is okay, for a moment.*

He's looking far off, in an absent kind of way. *Dad, please come back.*

He's an immaculate dresser, and I stare at his dark blue wool suit accented by the pale lavender of his shirt. Always inspired by luxurious details, my eyes admire his royal blue silk tie and deep purple handkerchief in his breast pocket. I hope to one day understand the formula for such elegance. He looks beautiful and pathetic, like a wilted flower.

I can smell it on him. Sick with concern, my insides begin to cave like a tall building collapsing on itself.

"Have you been drinking? Dad? Can you hear me?" I beg, naively convinced he can help us out of this. *What am I supposed to do? This feels impossible.*

"Requirement" by Grandma Margaret

I need to know
That which my skin can feel
as love.
I need to hear the sound of it;
A sound like sunlight
on green leaves.
I need to be rooted in the earth;
swinging with the tides;
part of the sun, and the shadow of night.
Surrounded by that essence of relationship,
Which, unspoken,
Speaks to every sense;
The world opens,
All needs are nourished,
And from the chrysalis you came
A full size human.

CHAPTER 34

QUIET DEVOTION

It's not something I experienced much as a child; parents who held me consciously.

I am a different parent to my kids, interested. Even when we don't have the words to talk about our wounds, we find other ways. It takes time to heal. We bury stuff until we are ready to shine a light on it. Our pain can erupt with or without sound.

"Frankie?" I say, gently pushing the door open a bit, unsure of what I might find. I look at her version of organization as my eyes scan her room, piles of clothes strategically situated depending on where they are headed: soon to be worn, washed, or put away. She's seated in her favorite chair looking at herself in the mirror.

How I remember those days, fascinated with the reflection of my expressions. Sometimes when I would cry, I'd run to the mirror to see what was happening.

Looking at my daughter now, I take in her long, blond hair, a golden cape of varying yellows. I see her frown at her reflection and wonder what she is thinking. *Will she let me hold it too?*

I appreciate how she's changed over the years. Frankie used to be swift and clunky, her spitfire energy whirling her around so she'd lose her balance only to jump up and say, "I'm okay!" Now she possesses a grace born from an ancient elegance, almost regal in the way she tends to herself. Admiration courses through me as I look at her.

My quiet devotion is short lived. Anger sits in my stomach. The "WTF" attitude possessing me is my cue to know I am taking it personally, once again lost in a thought process that has me blaming myself. *Why is this happening?*

She sees my reflection in the mirror, and we lock eyes. Our steady gaze is both connected and distant. Facial features change. My smile is meant to soften my confusion. I'm not sure it works. Hers is filled with concern, still frowning. Lovely blond brows knit together, and her bright blue eyes darken.

Message received. She wants to be alone. My need to know why she's drinking persists. I smell fear leaching from my pores.

She spins in her seat, looks at me sheepishly, and moves to her bed. She designed it herself, measured and configured all the details. It's tall, with a tunnel-like hiding space underneath, lined with cubbies. For a short while the elongated cave had twinkle lights and pillows; today, it doubles as a shoe closet. I sit at the far end to give her some space.

I sense a rebellious mischief coming from her, like she can pull one over on me. I get it. I can be slow on the uptake. I mean, hey, she took a bottle of wine from the kitchen, opened it, and drank it, under my nose. *Clearly there's some stuff I just don't want to see.*

"Hey," I say. "Have you been drinking?" I smell the red wine in the room and suspect she poured it into one of the open containers placed on her bureau. My favorite pinot noir is made by Meiomi, rich and full bodied like a cabernet. I'd know it anywhere.

"No," she says, swallowing a smile and turning away from me. It never gets old, this talent my daughter has with finding joy in every moment—especially when I am upset. She has pushed my buttons and relished my reactions for years. More times than not, she has to turn her head away to hide her hilarity. This is a game we play, one of our many expressions of love.

"What's going on?" I say casually. My voice is a little too high, which shows I'm nervous.

"Nothing, Mom," she says with a sigh of irritation. My eyes stay with her. "I'm bored," she offers. She drops her head into her pillow and looks at me from the corners of her eyes, waiting for me to do something, I guess. I feel unprepared.

"Yeah, boredom—it's a doozy," I say, moving a little closer and placing my hand on her leg. She doesn't move away. "It's the place we go when we've lost touch with our imagination. How are you feeling?" I ask, hoping she will tell me. I feel sadness between us, which lets me know I need to be gentle and soft. I close my eyes for a moment. *I'd rather be doing dishes, anything practical and unemotional.*

The theme for my yoga class today was "breathe and be." I asked students to stay with whatever shows up, sensations and feelings both, three rounds of breath minimum. The focus was to notice when you want to run and, instead, change your mind.

Well, here I am, breathing.

I stay and make myself available to hold her hand, literally, if she lets me, and metaphorically if she doesn't want to be touched. As we sit quietly together, everything begins to shift.

Frankie starts to cry and turns her head toward the windows in her room, away from me.

"Sweetheart," I say. "Tell me what is happening. Let me feel it too."

"Let me think about what words I want to use," she says, keeping her head turned.

"Okay," I offer in support.

"I don't know, Mom, it's just hard sometimes. Drinking makes me feel better."

"I understand," I whisper, wishing I knew what to do. All these emotions that make no sense sometimes are meant to be experienced, fully. We just need to express them. I feel inadequate and, like her, just want them to go away. My realization upsets me.

"Mom," she begs, keeping her head away from me. I wait. Then she says, "I'm a terrible sister." I can barely hear her mumbling into the pillow, but she says it again, firm and clear. "I am a terrible sister, Mom, the worst."

Her words are heavy. I have no idea what she is talking about. My eyes move to the windows behind her. It is still daylight as the wind blows through the trees in the garden. *I wish I could fly.*

"Why do you say that, honey?" I sing softly in her direction.

Her face turns slightly toward me, her eyes clenched tightly. "I just sat there when Dad hurt him. Not once did I try to stop it. I never did anything. I just watched." The wails begin with her mouth wide open and smashed into her pillow. I pray it will ease the truth of what she carries.

"Oh, Frankie," I say hopelessly, knowing well her pain is big. It feels like a guilt borne from a place of thinking she could have prevented it from happening.

"I did nothing," she whimpers. I move a little closer to lie next to her, and she lets me. I gently place my hand on her warm back, heaving with sobs. United in sadness, I connect with her anguish and confusion, let it surround us like steam from a sauna, and refuse to let go.

By allowing me to be with her, something opens. Moments like these help me know what kind of mom I want to be and are a source of strength and compassion.

Frankie falls asleep, and I stay with her, our bodies warmed by our closeness.

I remember being her age when I first got drunk. I was with Dad at a reception for the new theater opening. In my effort to clean up after patrons, I swallowed whatever they didn't finish. I laugh to myself now. *I was a swill drinker from the start.* I have no idea why I did it; maybe it was curiosity. When I look back on that time in my life, I remember being miserable all the time. I thought I was ugly, weird, unloved, alone, and lame. *Preteen hell.*

Dad took me home, put me to bed, and I eventually got sick. He was gentle and kind. *Was I unconsciously trying to be like him? Is that possible?* He didn't ask about my choices. I don't even know if he ever told Mom. *Did my state scare him? Was he ashamed?*

What I consider disregard, the lack of conversation surrounding the incident, annoys me. He took no measures to understand my motives. *Wouldn't that be useful, for both parent and child?*

Frankie's eyes flutter, and a slight groan leaves her lips. It feels good to be close to her right now.

"Hey," I say gently.

"Just tired, Mom," she says looking at me with her blue eyes. "I'm sorry. I don't know what I was thinking. I just wanted those feelings to go away," she admits.

"Yeah, I understand."

"Mom, can we talk about this later? I just want to sleep."

"Sure, Frankie. I love you." I slide out from next to her and kiss her forehead. She smiles when I do this, and I smile back, even though she can't see me.

"I love you too, Mom. And thanks for being here. I'm better now, sort of, I think."

My smile turns a little sad as I wonder if we will revisit this conversation. Feeling some of her pain knocks me flat. I move myself out of her room to let her sleep.

Surprisingly, I am not tired. My head is spinning with thoughts and memories from the past. I settle into the emotions I had when visiting with my dad in the new theater so long ago. The theme of being lost is strong.

I think about how easy it is to disappear from my own life, those joyless periods comprised of the bare minimum, when I choose only to exist and take my heartbeat for granted.

What structure supports a living, maybe even thriving, reality? Is it a mindset? Being curious leads me to discovery. Maybe that is all I need.

Dad lost his way long before he died, just after the new theater was built. He remarried and pretended to care but couldn't swing it.

I remember visiting him at the hospital. Looking back, I suspect he did not want to be found. *I think he was saying goodbye.*

"Life Cycle" by Grandma Margaret

Autumn, exhaling summer,
Wrinkles the land with its dry breath.
Yet my mind moves circularly,
And I'm renewed in autumn
as in spring.
The wind, whirling here its ochre leaves,
Flies on to a far place,
where, rustling in silken green,
It smells of flowers.
Today is seeded with tomorrow.
Memories, transmuted to hope, carry their summer
fragrance
into the fire I light tonight.
I rake the ashes
to spread upon the garden;
And gather wood from a felled tree.

CHAPTER 35

MWL (MEMORY)

We miss school for an entire day.

Mom flies me and my brother down to Santa Maria to visit our father in the hospital. He's been admitted to the intensive care unit. He collapsed during a performance in which he plays a character named Dr. Gerald Lyman from William Inge's *Bus Stop*. I have the review in my pocket, and I read a small section of it repeatedly, even though I don't understand it completely.

> Only Michael Leibert manages to penetrate very deeply into character; his rumpled academic Lyman is achingly realized, a man whose high, sensitive intelligence has only made him the lonelier. Leibert's Lyman walks through life as though it were a sewer; the keenest irony in this play is that no one else in the diner recognizes the soulfulness of someone capable of observing that "maybe in evolution, man has passed the place where love exists" (Christon 1984).

A nurse takes us to meet with a doctor who tells Mom that Dad has an abscess on his liver. We follow him through double doors and behind a curtain to find our dad surrounded by beeping machines. He looks puffy, swollen, and jaundiced.

His sad eyes merge with a half-smile in greeting, making him seem hopeless. He wears a look, like a solemn vow, that tells me he is fated to be here. It pisses me off. My anger prompts my chatter as I desperately and unsuccessfully try to change his resignation. His disappearing act started a few years ago, but all my seventeen-year-old love wants to save him, for myself.

"Dad, c'mon. You have to get better. Fight. It's too soon for you to die."

"Meighan, I am so tired."

"If you die, what's going to happen to me? I need you. Doesn't that mean anything?"

He reaches out his arm toward me, and I take his hand, soft and warm.

"Who's going to walk me down the aisle when I get married? Please don't go." He closes his eyes, and my heart sinks.

I leave Dad's hospital room, crouch on the floor of the corridor, and try to cry.

Held by frustration, I can't release myself in sorrow. Unable to reach him is the truth that strangles me. My powerlessness is suffocating.

We fly home. Neither my mom nor my brother knows what to say. We seem to be in a fog of shock, seeing him so close to death. The next day, in great surprise, we receive news of Dad being discharged from the ICU. This is a good sign as it means he is getting stronger. We gratefully go on with our lives and await his return.

I'm watching TV and eating potato chips in Mom's bed. It's after school, early evening. Mom's out on a date, and the phone rings only forty-eight hours since our return.

"Hello?" I say, irritated and not wanting to be interrupted from watching my show.

"Meighan?" she says. "It's Grandma Margaret." She pauses.

"Hi, Grandma," I say happily. I envision her sweet smile first. She has a tremendous talent for baking. We share a name in common, Williams. It's her maiden name, the one she grew up with: Margaret Williams. When she married Grandpa Grant, she added Leibert. My dad was born Michael Williams Leibert, and I am Meighan Williams Leibert. Our initials are both MWL. Her voice sounds worried.

"Your dad is dead. He died." She begins to cry. "I'm so sorry. I…" She can't continue.

"Oh *no*," I wail. *I thought he was getting better. What does this mean?* I start screaming. I'm holding the receiver away from me. My brother runs into the room, and I give him the phone. I turn around and bury myself into the blankets and pillows on Mom's bed. *What is going to happen to me?*

One article reports his cause of death as complications after abdominal surgery at the age of forty-four, with no mention of alcohol.

Dad's death proves he didn't love me, certainly not enough to stay alive. I know this to be true. It travels through my body like a freight train, fast and determined. First the theater and then the booze. Here we are, entrenched in *his* way, the ultimate sign that I do not matter. I allow his passing to leave me rudderless, adrift, and, lost.

As I sit with this memory, I broaden my impression of what happened to him. Dying alone feels tragic, a strange plight for a man who built a life and career around connecting people. *Without the theater, who was he?*

In 1982, the BRT received sixteen awards from the San Francisco Bay Area Theatre Critics Circle, no small feat. Maybe that was enough for him, the pinnacle he'd imagined for himself. Later that year in December, Dad took a year's sabbatical for personal reasons, no doubt to get a handle on his drinking. On August 10, 1983, the local newspapers report his resignation from the BRT. The Board of Directors said it was voluntary, but Dad refused to comment. I find this suspicious.

I imagine he had nothing to say. What must it have felt like to be rejected by his child?

I spend the next few hours reading *Bus Stop* to understand my dad's character. Convinced he chose the part on purpose, I am curious about his final character.

Lyman too is an alcoholic, a failed academic professor who likes to go after young girls and can't seem to keep a job. Lyman slowly loses his ability to hide from himself, forcing him to take a hard look at the man he has become.

Without the Berkeley Repertory Theatre, who was my father?

Lyman says, "I have disapproved of my entire life...but I suppose I couldn't resist living it over again" (Inge 2018). I think about Dad, after reading this line, and imagine he felt similar. Much of his life was filled with wonder and magic. How could he not want to relive it?

With his death I lost all the dreams I unconsciously weaved into the fabric of our father-daughter relationship. A part of me got buried alongside him because I didn't, nor did anyone in my immediate circle, possess the necessary tools to help me mourn him. Gently reliving our past while asking his other family to help me know him better, to share their experience, makes me not feel so alone. This gives me strength to revisit my own forgotten moments, the ones I don't like to remember.

"Untitled" by Grandma Margaret

The telephone rings in an empty house.
Ringing, ringing—like a voice
screaming at the sea,
or a letter, unopened.
I listen, and it frightens me.
What words are hushed before they're spoken.
What hand not taken?
Who left alone?

CHAPTER 36

LOYALTY

Tony Amendola is an actor, a forty-year veteran of film, TV, and stage. Film credits include *Blow, Annabelle*, and *The Mask of Zorro*, and TV credits include *Black Bird, Stargate*, and *Once Upon a Time*. Despite his success in Los Angeles, Tony has never forgotten his roots in the theater, especially in the BRT.

His email arrives in the late morning, but I don't see it until early evening. By this point I've resisted reading these wonderful messages on my phone to enhance the experience. In my heart they deserve my full attention, so I do my best to set the stage. I take my computer into the garden. Vespa sits by my feet. The late summer climate gives me enough light and warmth to feel comfortable without a sweater. Hot tea warms my insides.

> I first met Michael Leibert in 1978. It was a fortu-itous meeting, especially for me. Actually, what I first noticed about him was his unusual laugh. It was like a marriage between three staccato puffs of air and a strong barrel-chested baritone. We met at the Oregon Shakespeare Festival. It was my first professional job out of school, and I was performing in a play about the

playwright and misogynist August Strindberg. It was a funny play, no doubt, but the laughter coming from this one theatergoer was particularly raucous and helped fuel that evening's performance. The stage manager Jeffrey Hirsch introduced me to Michael, and we had breakfast at Hamlet's Roost shortly afterward. Michael immediately struck me as being sophisticated, erudite, and a worldly man of the theater. He had an easy manner and was comfortable to be around.

He told about his plans for his theater in Berkeley, his hope to expand the acting company and his desire to have me be a part of that expansion. However, what he said next really floored me. He told me that if I agreed to join the company, he expected a five-year commitment on both our parts. I nearly spat out my coffee. It was only later that I realized that loyalty and a belief in company was the heart of his artistic leadership style. Little did I imagine that a five-year commitment would result in a ten-year stay at Berkeley Rep—a ten-year stay that shaped and challenged me as an actor, as a director and as a human being; a ten-year stay that is the bedrock upon which I've managed to build a career that has stretched over forty years. So, some of the words that come to mind when I think of Michael are loyalty, support, and vision.

Tangible proof of his leadership and vision survives today on Addison Street in Berkeley. He started a small storefront theater on College Avenue and grew it until it was one of two flagship theaters in the entire Bay Area. His supportiveness and generosity toward me personally manifested themselves in some very odd casting including his wish to see me play the Gentleman Caller in Williams's *The Glass Menagerie.* I thought it was madness, but he insisted, and, as usual, he was right and that performance turned out to be one of my favorite experiences at Berkeley Rep. His patience and belief as he guided me through that performance is where our friendship really deepened.

Occasionally, on a really magic night in the theater, when the audience is heaven and everything flows effortlessly, I sometimes think I can still hear his laughter—three short puffs of air married to a strong baritone—and I whisper to myself, "Thank you, Michael."

"Loyalty, support, and vision" are what Dad delivered. They are the pillars for his success, the foundation for his theater, validated by a ten-year commitment.

These trademarks of Dad are not unfamiliar. I infuse them into my parenting, and they are fundamental qualities in my triad. I decided long ago I must make the most of the time I have with my kids living with me under one roof. I tell them often, "When you move out, you get to call the shots. Until then, I need you to be open to all my suggestions. My job, as I see it, is to provide you with as many experiences as possible, so you are well-equipped when you venture out on your own. You don't have to like any of it; you just have to be willing to taste it."

That's *my* vision, and it is best executed when I am supporting my kids in a healthy way. Giving them room to make their own decisions will ensure we continue to learn from each other.

"Winter Night" by Grandma Margaret

The rain rattles in the down spouts,
And clatters like a torrent of gravel
Against the window.
I lie and listen to the violent night,
Remembering a storm's passion
matched our own,
In thunderous accompaniment.
Now it's just a hostile hand,
hurling pebbles at my loneliness.

CHAPTER 37

PITY

I wake up to find a note, neatly folded, on the floor near my
bedroom door. I open it and read:

> Dear Mom,
>
> I already feel real bad and embarrassed for what I did.
> I'm truly sorry. I don't know what's wrong with me or
> why I feel so sad sometimes. I love you, Mom, and I
> promise to do better.
>
> Love, your daughter,
> Frankie

What scares me? Thinking I don't know how to support her.

"Frankie," I say walking into the kitchen. She's pouring milk
into her cereal bowl. "I got your note. Thank you for writing
it. I can only imagine how you might be feeling."

"Yeah," she says looking up. "It's hard to describe." I see tears in her eyes, and her face flushes. "I don't like talking about it, Mom."

"We don't have to," I assure her. "Just know I'm here. And maybe we can do something else, like go to the beach or jump out of an airplane."

"Really?" she says, and her face brightens. She is forever the adventurer. Maybe that's all we need, to find ways to play together. On our drive to school, she's abuzz with ideas of fun things we can do, and I try not to give in to my fear of missing out on something practical, like paying a bill. *My seriousness is such a killjoy.*

In my yoga class I set the theme of "not caring." Why be attached to what happens or doesn't happen? I suggest to students to create a space where everything is welcome: the irritation, the frustration, the strength, the flexibility, the desire, the judgment.

"Look at your self-talk. Is it supportive? Try 'wow' or 'yes.' My idea is to explore commitment without expectation."

I think about this after class and hope I might be able to do the same with my kids—not care what happens and love them anyway.

A package sits on my stoop. It's a big box from my dad's second wife, Kimberly Kay King. We connected via email and telephone a few times in happy reminiscing. For her, as an actor, being a BRT company member was a dream come true. Falling in love with Dad was an additional bonus. They were married for a brief time in the early '80s. She sent me his favorite cooking spoon, a cast iron pot, and a copy of an educational film they made together, playing themselves, about the nature of alcoholism, titled *Promises: Profile of an Alcoholic.*

Dad admitted himself to several treatment programs during their marriage. I recall having dinner with him and Kimberly the night he told me he was an alcoholic. I was thirteen. When I asked him the next day about the bottle of brown liquor I found in the back seat of his car, he told me it was medicine. These memory flashes give me a better idea of the slippery slope he was on.

Maybe this film will give me some answers. What I hold in my hands feels more precious than the box I got from Susie years ago.

I put the pot and spoon on the stove and think about cooking stew for dinner. Then I move to the couch, slip the thumb drive into my computer, and hit play. *What will you show me, Dad?*

The story begins on stage, actor Kimberly and director Dad discussing a scene. *There he is.* It's like yesterday. Seeing him and hearing his voice trigger emotions. I have tremendous love for this man. I feel it everywhere. I am connected to him, without question. I sense pride too. He is my dad.

The film portrays Dad's drinking as an issue in his marriage and work. In the opening scene, Kimberly and Michael leave the theater, lightly bickering. Dad says reassuringly, "No, it's not…it's going to be fine…would you just trust me? Trust me, trust me" (Leibert 1982). Later at home, over dinner, Kimberly asks him not to drink and says, "You promised." Dad responds, "I know what I promised. I told you no more hard liquor, a glass of wine with dinner, maybe a beer now and then. I haven't had anything to drink for a couple of weeks" (Leibert 1982).

He plays a man deep in denial, and it makes me wonder how close to the truth his role must be for him. Throughout the film, I sense he doesn't believe he has a problem. Even when he's sitting in an office discussing treatment options, I hear him say, "Maybe I need a drink every now and then. That's just normal" (Leibert 1982).

I watch him dismiss Kimberly's concerns with tireless excuses. She struggles with his lies and broken promises. She busies herself throughout the film, covering for his inability to show up and function. *I know this experience.*

One night, he's at the theater reading, making notes and working his way through a fifth of bourbon. He steps slowly onto the stage, leans into his glass as he places it on the bar, and turns to scan the empty seats around him, imagining applause. He then pulls a book from his pocket and begins reciting a passage from Eugene O'Neill's *The Iceman Cometh*. I listen to the words:

"Of course, I have pity. But now I've seen the light, it isn't my old kind of pity—the kind yours is. It isn't the kind that lets itself off easy by encouraging some poor guy to go on kidding himself with a lie—the kind that leaves the poor slob worse off because it makes him feel guiltier than ever—the kind that makes his lying hopes nag at him and reproach him until he's a rotten skunk in his own eyes. I know all about that kind of pity. I've had a bellyful of it in my time, and it's all wrong!...I don't blame you. I know from my own experience it's bitter medicine, facing yourself in the mirror... I'm just an old man who is scared of life, but even more scared of dying. So I'm keeping drunk and hanging on to life at any price, and what of it? Then you'll know what real peace means...because you won't be scared of either life or death anymore (O'Neill)."

I rewind to watch and listen several more times. I collapse with a truth that seems impossible to hold: Dad made this film to tell the world *he doesn't give a damn.* If facing himself in the mirror was in fact "bitter medicine," he quite possibly sought the only relief he could find by drinking himself to death.

The film ends with Kimberly handing him his suitcase for a treatment stay. Dad turns to look solemnly at the camera. He just stands there without an inkling of hope, his eyes steadfast in resignation. I now remember the goodbye I wouldn't accept so many years ago, something that sounds like, "This is it. I'm done."

I do not want to give my children broken and empty promises.

As a child I kept thinking the tall people in my world were dependable, even when my experience told me otherwise.

My belief they would be *if I was a good girl* was enough to keep me trying.

Until now, I did not understand the impact of my dad's actions. At the time, the pain of loss left no room for investigation.

I want to show up fully for my kids, even when it's messy and I'm scared. They need to know that in my darkest moments, I have their backs. My patterning runs deep, and I can forget to pay attention. But I also know I can change.

Love is all encompassing. It is never a "sort of" situation. You're either in or out. If I can't love myself, it is unlikely I can love another. I sit with this for a while. It knocks me flat and makes me less confused.

Maybe Dad did not love himself and was blinded by his own insecurity—"scared of life but even more scared of dying. So I'm keeping drunk" (O'Neill). Is drinking where Dad felt safe?

Al-Anon taught me to take it easy and be gentle with myself. I learned that where I put my attention matters. I absolutely want this "knowing" for my kids.

Feeling insecure kept me hidden for a long time, secretly wishing I was different.

"Two Summers" by Grandma Margaret

Most days that summer when I was thirteen,
I sat high on our cherry tree,
Hidden from my family,
And closer to my dreams.
In that green bower, hung with rubies,
As the long, hot, fragrant hours slipped swiftly by,
I read about life, and love, and beauty,
And wondered when it might begin.
Unaware of the sunlight, warm on my bare skin,
Or the scratch of bark against my back;
I left the sweet, red fruit, untasted too.
And though my mouth was dusty with desire,
The sky open to infinity above me,
I slaked all thirst, and wondering,
with words.

I swim naked in the tideless pool.
My mind floats in my head
As my body in the water,
All thought suspended.
Beating in every crack of skin and consciousness,
Multiplied, misplaced,
My heart runs through me
to the warm green water.
The sun, melting my flesh,
irradiates the dark within;
And for a moment,
Extending, timeless moment
I am one with the sea, and the light,
And it is real.

CHAPTER 38

LANYARD (MEMORY)

I move to Berkeley to live with Dad when I'm ten because I'm flunking fourth grade. My new school, The Academy, will help me be smarter. It is seven blocks from our home, where we live in an apartment around the corner from the theater.

Dad walks me to school every morning, and I never want to go. Kids are mean. "It's easy," he tells me, "just a straight line from our apartment." I try my best not to show my upsetness, but I can't help it.

Sun streams through the trees, making the sidewalk sparkle. I hold his hand while I jump from one golden section to another, keeping my feet off the leafy shadows.

In no time, much to my dismay, we stand in front of the gated entrance. My tears won't stop. I am surprised by my crying because I don't really want to cause trouble. But going inside is absolutely the last thing I want to do.

"Please, Dad, please...don't make me go inside...let me come home with you...I can't do this. Please. I promise to be quiet, to be good. You won't even know I am there. *Please!*" I plead.

"Meighan," he says calmly.

Why doesn't he just say yes? Can't he see how sad I am?

"This is what you need to do. You go to school, and I go to work," he says.

"Can't we come back tomorrow?" I beg.

"Little one, this feels hard, I know, but it will get easier." *No it won't. Nobody likes me.*

His soft hands, entwined with mine, remind me of my lanyard key chain—connected, strong, unbreakable, a symbol of home. *I just want to be in your pocket, Dad. Please don't let go.*

He gently untangles his fingers, leaving my hand to hang disconnected. He assures me everything will be okay. Achingly, I watch him leave and then turn to take my own steps in the other direction.

My small classroom only has ten other kids in it—six boys and four girls. I'm too uncomfortable to pay attention to the teacher, but I try. My head just keeps thinking about other stuff, like being at home, alone. *Anywhere is better than here.*

The bell rings to tell us it is time for lunch. All the kids go outside into the yard to eat. I find a bench at the far side and sit in the sun to unpack what Dad made for me.

Dad knows how to put love into a brown paper bag. My thermos is filled with chicken vegetable soup; he cooked it for hours. The whole apartment filled with the aroma of thyme and garlic and oregano. I have a thin tomato-and-cheese sandwich smeared with butter, cut into four sections, and wrapped in wax paper, I have a small bag of BBQ potato chips, a chocolate chip cookie, and a soda—Dr. Pepper, my absolute favorite. I spread everything out in front of me on the bench like a picnic and smile at the feast before me.

I try not to listen to the other kids, who point fingers and make fun. Hearing their whispers makes my tummy twist. *The new girl this, the new girl that. Look at what she's got. She's so funny looking with her braids and her clothes...* What is so strange about my lunch? Part of me wishes it looked like everybody else's.

I run home after school, so when I get in the door I'm sweating and tired. I slip into Dad's smoking chair. It's my favorite place to sit, like being in his lap. The dark brown leather, worn through to a lighter shade on the seat and where his head rests, cradles me like a hug. Alongside is a table that holds several different pipes, with long necks poking through holes and leaning in a stand. My fingers trace the carved structures as I inhale the stale scent of tobacco.

I close my eyes and curl into the chair. Ours is a home of pretend. I spend a lot of time alone because Dad must be at the theater. When he's home, he is always a little bit far away, preoccupied and distant. This is at the heart of my loneliness, so deep I'm not aware of it really.

I inhabit that tiny sliver of a space held between invisible and forgotten.

"Route #128" by Grandma Margaret

The sheep are shorn,
And the high grasses cut down.
Only heat flourishes here.
Bare, burnished hills.
Dappled like a Palomino,
Blaze above a thread of river.
Barns with winged roofs
are weathered silver in the sun.
Dry fields waver like water
in their mirage,
and pale, wrinkled sheep
stand about in knobby clusters,
under a blue white sky.
The sun's hand presses
hotly, hotly,
Only heat flourishes here.

CHAPTER 39

AEDIN

Remembering bits from my childhood explains why I felt lost and disconnected. My parents were busy. Being preoccupied with my own stuff while raising kids can distract me from what's most important.

We return to EQUUS in April 2021. My kids are older now. Sebastian is fourteen, and Frankie is thirteen. They are not exactly enthusiastic about following my lead. Sebastian would rather be in Bora Bora.

We rent a car at the airport, and while searching for our vehicle in the parking lot, I realize how drained I feel. All the decision-making, coordinating, and responsibility sit on my shoulders. Right now, I wish one of my teenagers could drive and pay for something. And as soon as the thought shows up, I feel bad about it.

"Mom," Sebastian says as we drive from the airport in Albuquerque, New Mexico, to Santa Fe. "Just look around, as far as the eye can see. Desert." He sighs heavily before continuing. And I join him. "Flat." He pauses for effect. "It's a wasteland. We could be in Bora Bora in our own private hut swimming in clear blue water. Why are we here?" He slumps in his seat and leans his head against the passenger side window.

As much as I love this boy, he can be a real pain sometimes. Then he adds, "How much is this costing you anyway? Mom, it is such a scam. This horse business isn't real. They just take your money."

I don't know where to begin. Maybe not answering would be best. And as usual, I take the bait. "Sebastian," I say on the end of a long exhale. "We only had a few days, and this worked for my schedule." The silence is heavy, giving me room to silently admit how much I would love to be in Bora Bora. Then it dawns on me, the perfect thing to say: "When you pay for it, you can pick the destination."

He groans and I say with enthusiasm, "I wanted to get out of town and do something new and different and learn something together, as a family."

Yeah, I think, *why are we here?* I had the idea a few months ago. A three-day visit to continue what we started in 2019. After everything we'd been through in the past year, I figured we could use the support. Sebastian's lackluster attitude is a real bummer.

This time, we are mobile and independent. Along with the car, we rent our own casitas across from the EQUUS property. We can tour the sights, make our own food, and binge movies as we like.

On the bright side, Frankie has grown out of her "I hate Mom" phase and she now holds the "awesome teen" title. These days, she is happy with any adventure.

My preoccupation with Sebastian's attitude eats away at me slowly. Two questions fill my head: *Why is this happening?* and *What am I meant to learn?* Nothing I do seems to breaks through my irritation.

He tells me before bed, "I'm not going tomorrow." It throws me into a tailspin.

"Sebastian," I say, "that is not an option."

I am forced to sit with my intense upset and discomfort. "What ifs" swirl through my head. My stomach knots, and I sit on the couch to slowly freak out internally. My fear is strong. Here I am, getting ready to work with horses. Pretending won't cut it. How I present myself will call my equine guide and initiate the lesson. The horses pick up on the incongruence immediately. I laugh and utter to myself under my breath, "Get ready for the truth."

I do my best to make our trip fun. I give both of my teens driving lessons and remind them, "Santa Fe roads are the best for this." Frankie is delighted with the opportunity, eager to explore being behind the wheel. Sebastian is a bit unsure, not as confident as his sister. I encourage him and give him room to discover for himself. What I like about this exercise is how relaxed I feel. I can sense I believe in their ability, and it assures all of us. This is what being a good parent is—clarity and calmness.

I play rap music each morning. My big idea is to meet them on their terms, give them the music they like to listen to while I make breakfast. I scheduled them a day of learning with the horses alone. It was Kelly's suggestion, something about giving them their own experience. I welcome the break. I have since joined another wisdom circle and look forward to spending time writing, reflecting, and sunbathing.

Once again, Sebastian tells me he will not attend and he doesn't feel like participating. I believe him and have no idea how to handle it. So I wait. And when it is time to leave, my kids walk out the door and work their way to the EQUUS ranch. I do not check up on them or make sure they arrive on time. I let all that go and put myself in my son's shoes. Maybe he is in a place where he wants to make his own choices.

On our last day, Kelly has a special exercise for us. She calls it liberty work—a connected expression built on safety and freedom. She asks us to pick our favorite songs, and we move outside the small paddock near the barn. Sebastian wants to go first and then Frankie. I am happy to go last.

I watch my children engage and relate with horses maybe ten times their size. I see their relational field as one. I video and witness everything I love most about my kids, their daring and innocence combined. I see how they are both brave souls, ready for the world, willing to show up. My heart fills with parental pride as I acknowledge my small part in carrying them for nine months. What a ride.

High on the coattails of their experience, I step into the arena with my new teacher Aedin, a young horse with a fiery spirit.

I go slowly and try to open my heart. It feels a little silly, but it is the only thing I know to do to get all of me on the same page. I am aware of my kids and Kelly, sort of, from my periphery. My attention is with Aedin. Music surrounds us. Time stops, and together, we move. It is playful, genuine, exciting, and filled with joy.

When the music stops, Aedin and I walk back to the gate where my children stand. My kids are behind me as we move through the barn until I feel Sebastian's hands lightly touch my shoulders. He spins me around, and I turn to see his face alive with delight.

"Mom," he begins eagerly, "watching you out there, well, it's hard to describe, I had a vision of you as a little girl." I do my best to concentrate. "Isn't that crazy? I mean, I know you as my mom and seeing you younger kind of blew me away. Honestly, I don't think I've ever once before thought of you as a teenager." I hear his words, but I am still floating and have difficulty letting them land. "Seeing you with Aedin, you seemed so happy, young even. I almost didn't recognize you." I focus on my eldest child's gray eyes. "Mom, I'm not kidding. It was amazing. And I need you to know how much I love you."

There it is. He wraps his arms around my body and pulls me close, and we embrace his words. The connection between us has always been there. Tapping into it or activating it was enhanced through our equine experience.

I can trust what is here. More importantly, I know my son will show up. Aedin taught me the importance of play, to release and let go. My tendency to take everything so seriously keeps me from living a fun life. Freedom is in the heart of joy. That's what I learned. And my son saw it.

Today I know my inclination to plant seeds in different ways is an expression of love. Whether it is easy or challenging, when my kids appear disinterested, any experience that provokes growth has value.

"Morning Meditation" by Grandma Margaret

Life slides past me
as sand slips through the kitchen timer
every morning.
The breakfast egg, once raw, is cooked.
The unfolding day, new and uncounted,
Has lost four minutes from its destiny.
To measure time at all is to capture change;
To mark what was
that is no more.
I can consider yesterday with some dispassion,
But the moment just now passed, or passing,
Taunts me with the possible
becoming impossible.
Snatches what might be
from my eager hands,
And turns it, even while I watch,
To that which was.

CHAPTER 40

BETRAYAL

We return home from Santa Fe and settle into our routines around work, school, and friends. My kids get an invitation to go camping and river rafting for a weekend, which means I will get some much-needed alone time. Frankie, surprisingly, is cranky about the trip and keeps asking me to join.

"Mom," she says, "please come with us. It'll be fun."

"Frankie," I say irritatingly, "the last time I went river rafting, I was your age and I didn't like it then, so I'm probably not going to like it now."

Her blue eyes widen with innocence. "I want to spend more time with you doing fun stuff. C'mon. It'll be great," she defends. I lean toward her and smile. Maybe it would be good for us...but rapids?

I can't quite tell what I see in her eyes. Is it desperation or something else? Could she really want to spend time with me? I don't buy any of it and give in to my suspicion. "Francesca, what the hell is going on?" I ask uninvitingly.

"Nothing," she lies. "I just think the trip will be more fun with you there." I can't argue with the sentiment, but the truth is I don't want to go.

In the last minute, someone gets sick, and I need to fill the seat. I resign myself to a short vacation, a few days in the country air camping near a river with two of my favorite people. I pack my journal, look forward to being in the sun, and prepare myself for a new experience.

Frankie gets her wish, and I am introduced to a timid version of her when we are around strangers. Something is off, and it keeps her close to my side, practically in my shadow. She doesn't want to go anywhere alone, like to the shower or the bathroom. As much as I inquire, press, and plead, she refuses to talk about whatever is bothering her. Luckily, being on the river alone in raft under the hot sun is a full distraction.

I will now attest river rafting is not my jam. After being told multiple times I might die if I don't do this or that—like fail to fall flat or dare to lift my oar out of the water—I become rigid in my commitment to live.

I spend four whole hours clenching my jaw and holding my breath. The surrounding beauty is completely lost to me as I am overcome with my checklist of dos and don'ts. Years of rumination finally come in handy.

My kids are springy, muscled, and exuberant. They are fearless and eager and ready for anything. Their excitement makes me jealous. *What's wrong with me?* My terror is all encompassing. I stay stiff while watching them laugh and fully engage. I don't know how to have fun.

Rollercoasters—no problem, sign me up. Navigating a rubber raft down a river with jagged rocks—no thanks. On our last morning, the day after I survived, I sit with my aching muscles in the warm sun, meditating and journaling while Sebastian and Frankie break down our campsite.

Over the following weeks, I keep a close eye on my daughter and prod occasionally. Nothing breaks until we are together in celebration.

We're at my mom's seventy-sixth birthday party when I watch the color drain from Frankie's face. I go to her and she refuses to talk, but she will not leave my side. She tucks her arm through mine. I have a terrible feeling, and the first emotion to arrive is anger. It's so thick I can't see past it. My concern is overwhelming, making it impossible to enjoy the festivities.

I lack the courage to leave early from the party and give my daughter my full attention. We hold hands, go through the motions of birthday fun, and count the minutes as they pass.

By the time we are in the car, it feels like a year has passed. We are both exhausted.

"Frankie," I say softly on the drive home, "please tell me what is happening."

"Mom, I don't want to talk about it," she declares, sinking down into her seat and turning her body away from me.

I'm afraid. Something is wrong, and I don't know what to do. We drive home without music, and I follow my thoughts like I am running after a bus I need to catch.

We settle into my bed for some TV time, and I decide to put my foot down. "You have to spill it, Frankie," I say, "It is the only way I can help you. Something has been off for a while now. Tonight's the night," I hammer.

"I can't tell you, Mom," she says with tears trailing down her cheeks. *Oh shit.*

"Francesca!" I repeat. I'm either standing up or sitting next to her on my bed. I can't seem to get comfortable in one spot. "You have to tell me." I sound like a broken record. I'm slipping backward into an old pattern. *Fuck.*

"I will write it on a piece of paper," she says finally, and I feel a rush of air exit my body. "And only if you promise we don't have to talk about it," she begs.

I hear these words, and my whole body goes cold. "Okay." I breathe in. "That works." I breathe out. "I promise," I say with heartfelt intent.

She looks up at me as I enter the room. All I see is my little girl, so small and innocent, under the covers. Her eyes, wet with tears, implore me to be gentle. I try to bring it down a notch, but I am freaking out. My insides are on fire. I hand her the piece of paper from my desk along with a pen. She sits up and begins to write.

"I don't know how to spell it," she says. These words break me. It's like trying to swallow marbles on a full stomach. I just can't do it.

My heart is screaming. *What the hell happened?* "Just do your best," I say, afraid to speak. I stop breathing when she hands me the paper. I read, "Jason touched me inapropately."

"Oh Frankie," I whisper while she cries it out. I crawl into bed with her and hold her close. Here we are, mother and daughter, weeping our way through the unspeakable. "Never again, okay? You never have to see him again."

"Really?" she whispers.

"Yes," I say.

Jason is a close family friend in his sixties. He has two daughters and a wife. We connected on a ski vacation with multiple families, years back. Our family friendship grew over time, after my divorce. Sebastian considered him a male mentor. His generous and playful nature seemed genuine. He gave my kids what I believed I couldn't—fun.

I break my promise. In the wake of reading what happened, I ask her more questions. I want details, and Frankie delivers, without hesitation, the exact date and time of every misstep, tracked and measured.

"He kept telling me they were accidents, Mom," she says, "and I believed him."

Until she didn't.

"Will you tell your brother?" I ask.

"Why?" she says, curling into me.

"So he knows, Frankie. What Jason did is terrible." I cannot imagine keeping this secret from Sebastian. *Who is she protecting?* I also know it must be her decision.

We wait two days. In that time, I meet with Jason at China Camp to hear his side of the story. We sit at a picnic table in the shade, surrounded by the beauty of my favorite place. Shock keeps me calm and unemotional.

He doesn't deny any of it. What surprises me most is his thinking I will understand. I swallow bile and listen.

"You are such a wonderful mom," he tells me.

My insides begin to knot. I let my nails dig into my palms. My fingers curl tightly as I remind myself to pay attention. I keep slipping away, wishing to be anywhere else but here with the man who hurt my daughter. *How could I let this happen?*

I try to focus as he continues, "...open to all things, forgiving and attentive. Surely you can appreciate..." I doubt my ability to endure another word. And then I remember, if I do not see this through, all of us will suffer. *Listen hard!*

He seems almost happy to have my attention, eager to explain. I hear what he says and realize it doesn't really matter. My daughter is my only priority. I am angry, want to hurt him, and know vengeance will not change what happened.

My body goes numb. I need to get home; I don't want to be here anymore. I stand and thank him for his time. He tells me he would do anything for me. His words hold no meaning. They hover around me only to be carried off by the wind.

I don't cry on my drive home. My anger pushes me forward, and I want to speak with my kids.

Frankie agrees to let me tell Sebastian, and we do it together. He immediately calls Jason and wants to hear the admission for himself. We stand in the hall of our home—me, Sebastian and Frankie—listening together.

"We trusted you," Sebastian says. "We loved you. How could you betray us like this? I will hate you forever!" He hangs up and looks at me and then his sister. Sebastian puts his arms around her. "I'm so sorry," he says into her hair.

The three of us sit in the living room to talk. I look around the room at all the photographs of family. Images of Dad are behind Frankie. Ours home is filled with color and art, and our family is splashed all over the walls in different ways. We are held by the love that came before, and we continue to grow.

We will make the decisions together. Frankie is wrapped in a blanket on the couch. She has an energy of strength and fear. She is clearly not comfortable talking about it, but she is interested in knowing what she can do.

"What if he does it to another girl?" asks Sebastian.

"Yes," I say, "very good point. If we stay quiet, that is most definitely a possibility. Here's the other thing. Secrets cause real damage. I'm not sure we want to live with this one. Regret is a killer."

"Regret for what?" Frankie asks.

"In a few years' time, looking back, we may wish we had taken a stand, to report a crime," I say miserably. And then I go for it. "Something like this happened to me when I was younger than you, Frankie. Nothing was done. I slept in a closet for months because it made me feel safe."

"Oh shit, Mom," Sebastian says, moving next to me on the couch. He puts his hand on my knee. I look to Frankie.

"I need you to feel safe Frankie," I say. "We can go slow to figure out what you need, okay?"

"Okay," she says, smiling. Then her face goes dark. "Will he go to jail if we report it?"

I shrug because I don't know. *I've never been the adult in this situation.*

"Do we tell family?" I ask them both. First Frankie says no. I let it sit for a moment before I explain again about secrets and then add confidently, "We are not sharing the information to embarrass you, Frankie. We are also not telling anyone what to do about it. We just want to let them know so they can make their own decisions. Okay?"

As I sit here with my children unwinding the horror. I realize how good it feels to share it and, more importantly, how much I need to show my daughter that when awful things happen to us, we do not need to pretend they didn't.

Frankie is open to trying various modalities for healing. Talk therapy is out, so we find other ways for her to process what happened. She integrates the fear and the pain of the transgression on her own terms.

Whatever my kids are going through, feeling it with them is a mandatory signature for our relationship.

"At the Beach" by Grandma Margaret

The smooth and castellated shapes
of chambered worlds, unseen till now,
of bones, and trees, or river beds
ridged from the years of water flow;
These I find, and hold, and keep,
Feel in my hands, and rearrange
with wonder, at the life they tell.
Sometimes a flower at my feet
will send so bright a message out
of crimson, blue, or yellow gold,
That I must sit and watch awhile;
Seeing the leaves and petals turn
As slowly as the sun; and then
take root and grow within me, too.

CHAPTER 41

TEEN WISDOM

We're in the kitchen preparing food, chicken roasting in the oven. I'm busy whipping mashed potatoes while Sebastian wrestles the salad. His phone distracts him momentarily but not enough for him to leave the room.

"Bro, don't worry about me. I am good," I hear him say. "Take care of yourself. You do you. If I don't want to hang with those kids because they make me feel uncomfortable, just let me be. We can hook up another time."

He repeats the message using other words, and my jaw falls open. His confidence in being himself is a strong presence in our household. The influence is real; it shows me I have a choice to *convert* my sense of inadequacy into something else. Maybe I too can be okay with me, as I show up.

"Frankie!" I yell, hoping it reaches her room. "Please come set the table." I pull the chicken out of the oven. Sebastian moves into the garden. I guess his conversation has now become private. My smile broadens as I acknowledge the comfort surrounding us.

Frankie bounces into the kitchen and inhales the aroma of roasted chicken sitting on the counter. Rosemary and garlic fill the air. "I look forward to having a boyfriend who likes to cook," I tell her, a familiar topic of conversation between us.

"Mom, if you want it you have to believe it," she delivers happily while grabbing utensils from the drawer.

The sunshine falling through the skylight dapples her hair and makes it glisten like shiny gold. Jewels of heaven are right here in my kitchen. I know what she is talking about. I emptied half my closet and an entire bureau in my bedroom two weeks ago, making room for my "future guy."

"Don't you know that?" she continues. "You have to act as though he were already here," she tells me sincerely.

"Yes," I say, "I do know that. Thank you for reminding me." My face hurts from smiling. I think of something I heard earlier in the day: We have to be the energy we want to attract. Then I take a big breath in and let it out slowly. How is it that this girl continues to impress and surprise? Is it TikTok or just teen wisdom?

I have nowhere to go. I am already here. I consider how my thinking has complicated my life, influencing my emotional body, ranting and raving through decades, focusing on what I wasn't getting.

Living is the gift. All my happenings, big and small, are guides. If I choose to pay attention, I will learn. If a reaction occurs, I will inevitably find myself in a repeat cycle.

I grew up obsessed with outward function, unconsciously thwarting my existence and making it impossible to find comfort. I created a pattern of hiding from myself to meet the needs surrounding me. Like every good girl, I wanted to help. I see now I was trying too hard.

Learning to see my sensitivity as a guide grows strength. Much of my childhood was spent embarrassed, maybe even ashamed for feeling so much. I didn't know how to handle it, leaving me lost and confused most of the time.

How I treat myself translates to everyone around me. I can *think* it is quiet, maybe even secret and only mine, but it is wholly not the case. My kids freak out when I flip my lid. It's a shared experience.

The more I lean into a relationship with myself and put aside all the cultural messages I've received along the way, the more I find clarity. My internal intelligence is a unique gift.

I spent most of my life running away from who I am. Working hard has brought me here, to a new sense of self that brings me joy. I am discovering how to appreciate me, as is.

I didn't have a real sense of safety growing up. I cultivated it post-divorce, for my tribe. I found love through parenting. My triad creates well-being together, which holds us when we get surprised and turned upside down.

"ON BEING TWENTY-EIGHT"
BY FLICKA MCGURRIN, 1973

CAN YOU BELIEVE
HOW HARD IT CAN BE?
DID YOU CONCEIVE
HOW HARD IT WOULD BE?
WHAT'S HAPPENING?
I'D LIKE TO KNOW.
WHAT SHOULD WE BE DOING.
TO MAKE US GROW?
IS IT HAPPENING RIGHT?
IT FEELS OKAY
SO SLOW. SO STRANGE.
SO MUCH DELAY.
HEAVEN SAY HELLO
SHOW YOUR CHARM
A HANDSOME FELLOW
WILL DO ME NO HARM.
BUT ALSO GIVE ME SOME STRENGTH WITHIN
TO BE FREE AND HAPPY
WITH MYSELF HEREIN.

CHAPTER 42

SECOND CHANCE

I get my curiosity and drive from my parents. They showed me, firsthand, how valuable it is to follow your dreams. My inability to acknowledge it before now is my fault. The legacy continues, and the pioneer spirit lives on. I have it from both sides, and I will honor it by passing it onto my own children. Dare. Be bold. Live loudly.

Relentless in my pursuits, sometimes I get what I want and sometimes I don't, and every time, I am stretched. Most of my life, I've wanted to be closer to my mom. I presumed this would show up as attention and her giving me something I needed. Not once did it occur to me my own strength could be the bridge.

It is 7:30 a.m. I am preparing for an online meeting as my kids head out the door to school. My phone rings, and I see it is my brother.

"Hey," he says. "CPMC just phoned. Mom had a heart attack last night." My head starts to spin.

"What? Where?" I say while slowly contemplating what this might mean. *Life without Mom. No, no, no, no, no.*

"She was in a wine bar when it happened. The manager phoned 9-1-1. She was admitted to the ICU at 8:00 p.m. I'm on my way to the hospital now." I can't read his tone. Shock has us both speaking matter-of-factly, our emotions halted. He gives me the floor and room number.

"Me too," I say, deciding I need to be there. "I'll meet you there." I grab my purse and move toward the door. I get to the car, Google the hospital for directions, and begin driving. *I'll tell my kids when I know something.*

I want to cry, but I can't. My fear has a tight grip around my throat. I've been here before when Dad was in the hospital thirty-eight years ago. I needed him to stay alive, as an expression of his love for me.

This is different. We have love. I know and feel it often. *Oh god. When did I see her last? What did we say to each other?* I can't remember. My stomach clenches.

Thirty-two minutes later, I see the emergency entrance of the hospital. *Do I go in there?* I park on the street and wait to feed the meter. An ambulance is parked out front. I walk up to the driver.

"Hi. I've never been here before. My mom was admitted last night. Do you know the best place to park?" It's hard to get organized when my feet are barely touching the ground. I'm in that weird place of simultaneously needing and not wanting to know what is happening. The longer it takes me to get upstairs, the more time I have to imagine nothing is wrong and vice versa.

"I'd try the garage," the guy in the passenger seat offers. "Just to keep your car safe. It's down there," he says, pointing forward toward the windshield. I follow his finger and look back at him. "Thanks," I say.

I go back to my car and drive down. The road is narrow and tight, and my tires screech on the turns. It is dark and cold. I park and take the elevator to the lobby, moving as if in a trance, to be approved for a name tag. *All these unfamiliar steps to find my mom.*

I hear the machines before I see them. My brother is sitting beside her. He stands up, and we hug. I turn to Mom, lying there, slightly off center, cemented. Everything drains out of me in an instant. I surrender to being completely lost without her.

Unconsciously, she calls me forward without hesitation. It is unexpected and immediate. Heavily sedated and intubated, she is destabilizing.

She is one of a kind, a blustering energizing talent of creativity, wisdom, and plain old fun, a painter, piano player, ocean swimmer, chanteuse, mom, grandma, cook, and entrepreneur. To be with her is a full flavor, a profound expression. Nothing is little about her. Over the years we have laughed, cried, yelled, and shut our lips tightly as we, very slowly, learned that family is the only structure needed to carry us through.

I lean over and kiss her forehead. I am reminded of the time she did the same with her own mother at the crematorium. "She's so cold" were the words she used, and the double meaning was not lost on me. In my thirties, I was afraid to kiss a dead body, but I did it anyway.

Mom doesn't feel cold, just stiff. It's unnerving.

I cradle her face in my hands and whisper, "What do you need, Mom?" The sounds of the machines continue beeping while I sit beside the woman who made me, holding what I can, desperately wanting to crawl up beside her. *Mom!*

The weight of worry, that nagging little concern, captures my breath. It carries me toward other looming thoughts like *Who will I be without her?* I keep bouncing back and forth between my fear and my faith. I don't want to get sucked into the depths of my despair. I prefer to stand strong in the midst of this massive shift we are experiencing together.

I drag my fear with me and think about who I want to be in this moment: a loving daughter, fully present. "Acknowledge what is happening, and don't run from it," I whisper to us both. Hers is a big personality, loud and boisterous, strong. It is not an easy task for her to let go. I suspect we are here because something needs to change. A hard stop like this is a real lesson.

My sister, brother, and I take turns. We commit ourselves to being with her all the time. She regains consciousness twenty-four hours after being admitted, and the breathing tube is removed a day later.

Her disinhibition, a temporary loss of the feelings that make her self-conscious, shows me a mom who is soft, gentle, kind, and openly loving. For days I have been swimming alongside her, with all the emotions she generates. This is not a familiar expression of our connection; we are usually guarded in our support of each other. This new version is precious amid the unknown. I listen and abandon myself to her lead. We continue our dance for three weeks. A friend tells me this is her *soul speak*—her true nature, unbridled, coming at me with armor down.

Mom puts her hand on my shoulder, pulling me close. "Meighan, are you happy?"

I tell her, "Yes." *Finally.*

Later she says, "I know you are a good mom. I trust your decisions." These are words I've waited all my life to hear.

Mom calls me on the phone when I am driving Frankie to school, "I just wanted to let you know where I am," she says. "I'm on vacation, and the hotel is really nice." Lost in time, she is unable to make sense of what is happening to her.

She asks, "Is this your house?"

I laugh, "No, not really."

She texts me at 4:00 a.m. "I don't want to bother you, but I really want to get out of here. I love you lots. Come visit soon." I text her back, "I'm your personal Uber. On my way." I don't know if she reads it.

Sitting with the possibility of my mom's death, holding it close, is terrifying. I do not feel ready.

I can easily step into a space where my need for her to be alive, for me, will drive me to misinterpret all of it, to take it personally. Today I am on a different path. I choose to stand beside her, to be in service as her loving daughter, which inevitably strengthens both of us.

This intense, heart-wrenching situation is not a story of scarcity or lack of worth or something I didn't get. It is one of love and life, filled with joy. Our appreciation for each other is abundant and seemingly endless. Her innocence is inviting and playful. I surrender.

This is uncharted territory. I trust her body will carry her through at its own pace. There is no rush now. I embrace the opportunity, the chance to reevaluate how I participate in my mom's life and what it means to me. I am not operating out of a sense of duty or obligation. I am tapping into a heartfelt desire to nurture, a redesign for both of us.

Mom is grateful for our attention. She smiles as she states, "I raised you all so well." She did. We are closer now, more connected together. I do not doubt any of it. This is where we need to be. I welcome what is to come, palms up and heart full.

Her recovery is overflowing with life and expression, hers alone. I'm in love with her, my mom.

I tried to escape it, *my family,* a few times along the way. I've had many periods where I thought I could live without them—daredevil moments, bold assertive acts fueled by my belief that I didn't belong.

My quest for more has been with me since birth. Coming home is a recurring theme for me. Inherently, I know that within the folds of our parent-child-sibling-business-family dynamic lies the heart of my purpose. My understanding and growth are planted here.

"Inner Journey" by Grandma Margaret

I travel half around the world to see
Fig trees,
and a convoluted coast.
Land and sea are similar everywhere.
Our needs discover novelty,
And distance creates distinction.

CHAPTER 43

WATERMELON

My family experiences throughout my life have delivered massive emotional moments. When I am willing to pay attention, they exist as true opportunities for me to further understand and comprehend myself.

I am a mom.

Allowing my kids to find their way gives me the room to do the same. The first part is familiar, I've done it since they were tiny with words like "just try it out." The second part of knowing myself took longer. Fifteen years of promoting my kids to be themselves have finally worked their magic on me. I am better at self-appreciation today, with less "supposed tos" and "shoulds."

Being a mom opened me up to what I needed from me: attention, love, and approval. We give and receive these qualities, and because of them, my kids reach out and ask for guidance. They want me to read their writings often, requesting feedback. They both say it this way: "Do not edit anything, do not change my voice, and make it yours. Just read it and report back what you think! If you make any spelling mistakes, okay, but otherwise, *do not edit*." They are in touch with their identities and aren't busy trying to be anything different.

None of the burden that influenced my childhood afflicts my kids. Their troubles, so far, do not emanate from self-sacrifice. On the contrary, they seem to be well-acquainted with their limits and hold strong to what works for them.

Frankie grabs a watermelon out of the fridge. She cuts it in half and inserts a straw. She carries it to the couch and places it on the coffee table. Beside it rests a spoon. She embodies enjoyment—easy and relaxed, almost blissed out. Her intuition is a combination of playful and practical efficiency. She is living inspired.

Jealousy is here a wee bit. I roll it around my tongue like a Tic Tac. This is a sheer moment of laziness on my behalf; call it a low-road expression because I also know my biggest joys are felt when I live out my dreams, however small.

I stop doing the dishes, let my jealousy slide down the drain with soapy water, and sit next to my daughter. We rub elbows and sink into this moment of comfort.

I'm not so far away anymore. I wound myself taut for decades, filled with unhappy feelings that only cinched me tighter. My life needs to be something other than just struggle. I know I am supposed to be more than a survivor. I get to be a leader too. I can make a mark that will be remembered by a few, maybe my kids.

Mutual participation inspires me. I have been singularly focused for too long. Sharing feels good. A team is appealing. The cooperation my kids and I create gives me a new flavor of family, sweet and tangy.

As I open myself up, truly and heartfully, my children have firsthand experience with my vulnerability. Inclusion is not burden; it is invitation. We are in this together. How can my life be wrong if I spend it with the ones I love?

I try not to judge my kids. Some days are better than others. In doing so, I become less critical toward them and myself. Here I can take responsibility and forge a reciprocal relationship in which we all contribute.

Frankie and Sebastian seem inclined to accept and appreciate themselves as individuals, something I did not experience at their age. They are wired for love—at least that's what it looks like from over here. My kids are showing the way. We are growing together. It is a beautiful and, at times, an unbelievable process. It knocks my socks off when they ask me what I would do or when they want my opinion about a decision they are making.

Today I try it out for myself.

It's Sunday, late afternoon, our theater night. We're getting ready to visit my dad's heart and soul, the BRT. I'm standing in the kitchen looking at my kids on the couch. My ten-day online immersion with psychologist and astrologer Debra Silverman ended a few days ago, piquing my interest in all things astrology. I share what's percolating.

"Hey," I say, wondering how they might respond, preparing for the worst and hoping to be surprised. I wait until they look up from their phones, then add, "I want to become an astrologer."

"Okay," says Frankie. "So?"

"Well…" I laugh. "I was wondering what you thought about that?"

Sebastian asks, "What's an astrologer?"

"I don't really know, yet." I emphasize. "For the past ten days I've been working a program that has me"—I swallow hard and sing while raising my hands in the air—"over the moon!" I laugh out loud and see toothy grins spread across their faces. "An astrologer is someone who understands the influence of the stars. It's an ancient science, the oldest around. The minute you are born, the planets form a signature, known as your natal chart. And from there, I can tell you all about you."

"Like what?" Frankie asks.

I love her curiosity and use it to get charged. "Like what you are here to learn, how you show up in the world, what challenges you, and what makes you thrive," I say excitedly.

Sebastian stands up and moves toward me. He sits in the tall chair near the counter and leans on his hands while asking, "Mom, what's really going on? What's the reason behind wanting to be an astrologer?"

I look at him and pray I can get this out in a clear way. "I've always been jealous of people who knew what they wanted to do. For instance, my dad's calling to be in theater was strong. He started performing when he was little. I have this impression that it would make my life so much easier if I just honed a skill. But I recently found out it is totally my nature to be a one-hit wonder."

"What's that?" they both ask in unison.

"Someone who completes something and is unlikely to repeat it and just moves onto another something. I'm like a goat who loves to run up the mountain, get to the top, then head down the other side to find another mountain to climb. It explains why I'm always finding new things to do." The Honolulu marathon and the Alcatraz swim come to mind, two big athletic ventures I only did once. *Done.*

"And?" my son pushes. *What is it with this kid?* I think. *Does he get his curiosity from me?*

"And"—I overemphasize while smiling—"I love working with people who want to know more about themselves. I think astrology will be a great addition to my coaching business. If I can fall in love with myself, I want to inspire others to do the same."

"Can you read my chart?" asks Frankie

"I don't see why not," I offer lightly, still unsure of what it all entails.

"Mom," Sebastian says, "I say go for it. If you're feeling it, just persevere. Don't let anyone squash your dreams."

Frankie chimes in. "Yeah, Mom," she says with her eyes shining. "We already know you can do anything. Every time you get an idea, you just make it happen."

"Really? That's how you see me?" I say somewhat surprised. Both my kids look at me with a facial expression exclaiming, "Duh."

This is a big moment. My kids are giving me not only approval but motivation too. I laugh to myself. *My cheerleaders.*

"Okay, then. Let's go," I say grabbing my purse. "Who wants to drive?" I hear their jaws drop behind me. "Just kidding!" I slide myself behind the wheel.

The BRT's production of Lucas Hnath's *A Doll's House, Part 2* sends me a message. Nora says to Torvald, near the end of the play, that she could not hear her voice. After slamming the door on their marriage and family, she spent two years alone to rid herself of those voices that did not belong. Eventually, she could hear herself.

Unlikely to leave my kids for twenty-four months, I listen to my voice through creative endeavors. I like to make stuff. "Period," as Frankie would say. Using my imagination and my hands, whether it be in the kitchen, in the garden, on paper or canvas, in knitting or needlepoint, in candles or creams. It can be anywhere in anyway. That's the beauty of my soul speak. It's limitless. Ideas pop into my head all the time. If I stay open to listening, my living inspires.

My dedication to figuring out how to make things is both exciting and fun. This is my happiness, and it is uniquely mine. It may not look like anybody else's. This is important to recognize because for a long time, I worried that something was wrong with me. It wasn't until I was able to be okay with me, entirely, that I stopped feeling broken. *My life is full of happy expressions.*

Ownership, choosing me and how I express myself, within the circle of family reinforces my lessons. I didn't have trust and responsibility growing up. That's why I felt so lost. I'm the only person who needs to believe in me. It's that simple. *My life, my way, with confidence.*

My unfolding began with my divorce. *What story am I holding, and am I willing to rewrite it? I was unhappy and unloved.*

"Let Us Fly Upward" by Grandma Margaret

Let us fly upward, open to the high winds.
Let us run to seed, and to flower;
To gold, singing in the wheat,
Or shadows that smell darkly purple.
Let us sweep the inky sea
with frills of white, or give her
Fog, as a shroud;
Muffling that moonlight voice.
Let us do anything
that is alive. Listen
to leaves, waking music with the birds,
And greet a new morning with your son.

CHAPTER 44

WITH HEART

Maybe I didn't have anything to smile about.

Most of my childhood photos reflect a pensive little girl. I look at these pictures with fascination and wonder where *my* seriousness came from. I look both innocent and unhappy. Even my mom remembers out loud, "You always looked so sad as a kid." Hearing these words reinforces my "mad," my believing I was a problem. Truth is, I didn't feel safe, plain and simple.

"Unloved" is the story that plagued me the longest. I wanted something from my parents they couldn't give me. But it didn't stop me from trying to get it, which caused a lot of suffering. It turns out, my parents loved me in their way, I just didn't like it.

Dad dying compounded my belief that I wasn't loved. His choosing the theater and the bottle over me was impossible to rationalize.

Mom would tell me, "Life is hard," and Dad often said, "Life isn't fair." I believed them. Their messages grew with me. The shared experience from one generation to another is important to acknowledge. I learned from my parents, and they learned from theirs.

I was loved in a way that didn't nurture confidence. Listening, considering, and appreciating are relationship qualities I did not experience growing up. It made me think nobody wanted to hear what I had to say. But it didn't keep me from trying. I just felt lousy doing it.

My inclination and desire to break with tradition brought me to parent differently. Accepting my kids wholeheartedly gave me a taste of the approval I've craved for decades, which brought me to love, in its purest form, for myself and them.

Reliving parts of my dad's life and finding new understandings of his values helped me claim my own. He was true to his sensitivity and used it to inspire everyone around him. His bravery motivated him to take huge risks on and off the stage. Anyone who knew him was better for it.

Dad writes in the program for the BRT's 1980 production of *My Heart's in the Highlands* by William Saroyan.

"I am one of Williams Saroyan's biggest fans. I have always loved his stories and plays. I find them full of exuberance. His tales of Armenian immigrants seem to me to be parables which address the plight of all spiritual exiles, anyone whose heart has ever been in the highlands.

Like the playwright, I have always been accused of being a sentimentalist. What's so bad about thinking with your heart? I'm a hopeless romantic. I believe passion and idealism is what theater is all about (Leibert 1980)."

Dad lost his way while enfolded in the arms of his theater family. He'd left his blood children long before. Discovering the truth can be terrifying. It wasn't until I reached my fifties that I realized his death had nothing to do with me. His life was of his own making, personally designed by a man who thought with his heart and lived that way too.

Today, I have a new version of Dad that offers me a different perspective than the one I formed as a teen. Hurt from childhood led to confusion as I grew older. Uncertainty convinced me something was wrong. Afraid to know myself, I let denial rule, until by some miracle, I lessened its grip.

His absence caused me tremendous pain. Without him I was left alone to wonder what I did wrong. My pursuit, over time, led me to find the man I didn't know. Appreciating all of him set me free. I cultivated a love expression, like trust, that nurtures and fulfills. It released me from holding on to what I thought I'd lost. Forgiveness is not hoping for a different past. It's accepting whatever you're given so you can know yourself.

Now I believe Dad pursued his dreams breathlessly, in part, *because* I existed. Having children can do that. Sometimes they inspire parents to go above and beyond. His greatest gift to me, received almost forty years after his passing, was his showing me the power of authenticity.

Dad's death was an act of surrender, by him and for him, beautifully because he didn't give a damn. It is remarkable to experience the wholeness surrounding an incident I interpreted as broken for so long. I can now give him the dignity he deserves.

I, too, want to live my life on my terms.

When I look at my life through the lens of loneliness, I see the conflict of *thinking* I didn't belong where I was, whether it be with my mother, my father, my siblings, my friends, or even my husband. I've come to understand everything I was looking for *out there* is already here, inside. I am my own resource. Being is belonging.

Dad and I are similar. I too am a romantic, a dreamer and quite sensitive. For years I dismissed and undervalued these traits. Now I hold them with great esteem. I've come to recognize I am powerful, sturdy, capable, and unique—a very different picture than the one I carried for so long, where I felt small, inconsequential, unloved, and replaceable.

I've learned I do not have to be defined by my past. How I choose to show up and my actions make me the person I am today. Remembering and reimagining will influence my present, maybe even my future, in a valuable way.

My capacity to welcome life as it shows up increases daily. As the matriarch of my tribe, I infuse a homegrown spice blend of loyalty, support, and vision. I no longer wake up at 4:00 a.m. on purpose and make time to go slower throughout my day. My children, Frankie and Sebastian, are wonderful role models who show me how to relax, stay true, and laugh often.

In discovering the man I didn't know, I somehow found a way to show myself the woman I want to be. This is the story I will continue to write.

ACKNOWLEDGMENTS

I woke up one morning with *The Man I Didn't Know* on my mind, and a few years later it became this book. In no way did I write this alone. These pages are borne out of many relationships, conversations, and experiences. A special warm gratitude hug to Jim Nisbet, Carol Collier, and Eddie Muller for inspiring me with their words and kindness. I am a lucky girl.

It is imperative I thank my early supporters, all of whom made this dream come true.

Adriana Pickering
Alistair Monroe*
Alta Phelan
Amy Blumenthal
Anne Swift
Art Boudrealt
Beth Fernbacher
Bill Atchley
Buddy Rhodes*
Carolyn Kemp

Christina Quezado
Christine Margetic*
Christopher Beasley
Craig Hartford*
Deanna Mooney
Deborah Johnson
Elizabeth Taylor Eckhardt
Eric Koester
Erik Lindquist*
Fiona O'Connor*

Flicka McGurrin*
Gina Baldanzi
Isaiah Fliessbach
Jaemie Altman*
Jamie Hascall
Jane Schopplein
Jeanie Piper
Jesse Henry
Joe Spano
John and Barron Leibert*
John Mitchell*
John Whitaker
Joy Carlin*
Joy D'Ovidio*
Karen Ingenthron
Karen Reynolds*
Kimberly Pearson*
Kit Canright
Lei Levi
Leslie Ades
Liam Hennessey*

Lili Wu*
Linda Marabito
Linda Wallgren
Louis Schilling*
Mark Madeo
Mary Christo-Crillo
McGurrin Leibert*
Mimi Halgren
Narsai David
Paula Marks
Peggy Knickerbocker
Rachel Kallok*
Richard Llora
Samantha Monge
Sara Whiteford*
Stephanie Handley
Summer Poole
Wayne Mullis
Winona Lewis
Yasmin Lambie-Simpson*
Zoe Kelman

*Denotes individuals who purchased multiple copies.

APPENDIX

CHAPTER 35: MWL (MEMORY)
Christon, Lawrence. 1984. "Trio of Dramas at Theaterfest." Stage
  Reviews. *L.A. Times*. August 9, 1984.

Inge, William. 2018. *Bus Stop*. Rockville, MD: Wildside Press.

CHAPTER 37: PITY
Leibert, Meighan. 1982. "Umatic 1 Promises, Profile an Alcoholic."
  Meighan Leibert. December 25, 2022. 31:52. https://youtu.
  be/2FP6pZkKhJU.

O'Neill, Eugene. 2020. *The Iceman Cometh*. Connecticut: Yale
  University Press.

CHAPTER 44: WITH HEART
Leibert, Michael. 1980. "My Heart's in the Highlands." Playbill,
  Berkeley, California, December 9, 1980.

ABOUT
THE AUTHOR

Meighan Leibert lives in Northern California with her son and daughter and their two dogs. She is a writer, painter, yoga instructor, personal life coach, astrologer, and HR manager for her family businesses in San Francisco: Pier 23 Cafe (www.pier23cafe.com) and Sweetie's Art Bar (www.sweetiesartbar.com). Proud daughter to pioneers Flicka McGurrin and Michael Leibert, she is raising her children to be confident and daring. Find more about Meighan at www.meighanleibert.com.

Made in the USA
Monee, IL
25 July 2023

39882523R00197